POSITIVE PARENTING

Discipline Your Kids the Loving Way

SIMON GRANT

© **Copyright 2019 by Simon Grant- All rights reserved.**

This document is geared towards providing exact and reliable information in regards to the topic and issue covered. The publication is sold with the idea that the publisher is not required to render accounting, officially permitted, or otherwise, qualified services. If advice is necessary, legal or professional, a practiced individual in the profession should be ordered.

- From a Declaration of Principles which was accepted and approved equally by a Committee of the American Bar Association and a Committee of Publishers and Associations.

In no way is it legal to reproduce, duplicate, or transmit any part of this document in either electronic means or in printed format. Recording of this publication is strictly prohibited and any storage of this document is not allowed unless with written permission from the publisher. All rights reserved.

The information provided herein is stated to be truthful and consistent, in that any liability, in terms of inattention or otherwise, by any usage or abuse of any policies, processes, or directions contained within is the solitary and utter responsibility of the recipient reader. Under no circumstances will any legal responsibility or blame be held against the publisher for any reparation, damages, or monetary loss due to the information herein, either directly or indirectly.

Respective authors own all copyrights not held by the publisher.

The information herein is offered for informational purposes solely, and is universal as so. The presentation of the information is without contract or any type of guarantee assurance.

The trademarks that are used are without any consent, and the publication of the trademark is without permission or backing by the trademark owner. All trademarks and brands within this book are for clarifying purposes only and are owned by the owners themselves, not affiliated with this document.

Table of Contents

Introduction 1

Chapter One: Understanding Parenting Behaviors 3

Chapter Two: Positive Parenting 7

Chapter Three: Communication 26

Chapter Four: Children's Behavior 38

Chapter Five: Positive Reinforcement 45

Chapter Six: Positive Discipline 76

Chapter Seven: Developing Resilience in Children 88

Chapter Eight: Preparing for Teens 110

Chapter Nine: Other Tips and Strategies 119

Conclusion 146

Introduction

Do you just wish your children would do what you tell them? That would be ideal, wouldn't it? In a perfect world, children would know what is best for them and make all the right decisions. You cannot achieve that level of control, but you can get close to it.

Parenting is no easy task, and it is a huge responsibility that parents have to bear. It is stressful, tiring, and time-consuming. There are many risks associated with it, too. If you parent improperly, you will raise a child that is flawed, one way or another. You don't want that, do you?

While parenting is never an easy job, it never has to be complicated. Parents fuss over how to address their children's problems and often choose the easy way out, which often cause negative consequences in the future. There are many effective approaches to raising children.

One of the most effective parenting methods out there is known as "positive parenting." Not only that, it is effective, but it is also very simple. This is what I will discuss in this book.

In this book, you will discover:

- How and why positive parenting works

- How to bring the best out of your children

- How to apply positive parenting in your home

- How to use reward systems to encourage good habits

- How to curb negative habits

And so much more!

Can you imagine it? Your children are listening to what you tell them, helping around the house, being social, and performing well at school, all of which achieved with little to no stress. No yelling, no hitting, and much positivity in the house. That can be achieved with positive parenting.

Intrigued? You should be. If you are ready to switch up your parenting style and are willing to put in the time and effort to apply positive parenting, then read on!

Chapter One

Understanding Parenting Behaviors

Parents around the world have three major goals: to ensure children's health and safety, to prepare them to live as productive adults, and to transmit cultural values, according to the American Psychological Association. Of course, these goals are ambiguous at best.

Parenting is an intimidating subject for every parent because it is a huge responsibility. How parents raise their kids will ultimately determine if the children will become the next millionaire or the next person to be a detriment to society.

We have yet fully grasped how our mind works, let alone how children development. Limited as we are, we can at least take previous practices from our ancestors and understand what works and what doesn't. This is exactly why there are so many studies out there that seek to understand psychology as a whole. For instance, a study by Aunola and Nurmi in 2005 shows that children internalize and externalize their mother's parenting behaviors, including how she displays affection toward and exercise behavioral and psychological control over her children.

There are countless ways to raise children, but let us classify them into four main parenting styles to simplify. They are authoritarian, permissive, uninvolved, and authoritative. All of these styles are based on two dimensions: warmth and control. Parental warmth is all about how parents show their affection and affection toward their children. How active parents are involved in the promotion of respect for rules and social conventions determine what is called parental control.

Authoritarian
Authoritarian parents exercise a high level of control over their children while offering little warmth. They are strict toward their children and have high expectations. Children often do not have much choice but to obey; talking back is not even allowed. Such parents often punish their children for poor performance. Such a parenting style often leads to hostility, delinquency, rebelliousness, antisocial aggression, as well as anxiety in children as they grow. Anxiety, in this case, could result from the fact that children lacked the opportunity to develop autonomy through the independent exploration of the environment. Depression is also linked to this style of parenting, as children received little to no warmth or acceptance from their parents.

Permissive
The permissive parenting style is characterized by a high level of warmth and a low level of control. In this case, the parents are more like a friend than a parent. That means children only have to follow a few house rules, have no expectations to live up to, and receive

minimal guidance or direction. Parents who raise their children this way tend to be very loving and nurturing. Children are often left to decide on their own when they have to solve their own problems. While the permissive parenting style gives children with affection and freedom, it has its downsides. It is hard to control children's behavior, which leads to a decrease in social competence and academic achievements. This parenting style often leads to bossy, dependent, and impulsive behavior in children as well as low level of self-control, academic achievement, and failure to learn emotional control and persistence.

Uninvolved

Parents who raise their children this way tend to exercise a low level of control and offer little warmth and affection toward their children. The parents do not use any particular discipline style, if at all. They are not interested in being a parent. Communication is limited, so children are left to their own devices. Children need their parents' affection and guidance, but uninvolved parents provide neither of them. This could lead to depression and other behavioral problems in children. As they become adults, they tend to display aggressive behaviors and perceive high levels of rejection, not to mention their inability to cope with problems effectively.

Authoritative

The authoritative parenting style is arguably the best way to raise children, as it offers a high level of warmth and control. Children receive a high level of affection as well as discipline, which opens up two-way communication and allows parents and children to work together toward a goal. Children who are competent, mature, assertive, and disciplined tend to be raised by authoritative parents. Such parents take a child-centered disciplinary approach to discipline and communicate with their children. From this, children could learn and grow exceptionally well.

The downside to this parenting style is its difficulty. It requires a lot of time, patience, and energy from the parents to pull this off. Plus, it is also situational. Parents who are living under stressful conditions such as poverty may not have the luxury to raise their children authoritatively and tend to use less effective but easier parenting practices.

The authoritative parenting style is also known as positive parenting, which will be the entire focus of this book.

Chapter Two

Positive Parenting

Most adults will become parents at certain points in their lives, and yet so many people have no idea how to raise children properly. In many cases, they cannot be blamed, as there are so many things to consider that they cannot be expected to make all the right decisions that would result in positive development in children.

Many of us strive to be great parents, but we are faced with confusion and frustration in our pursuit. Parenting is a serious commitment, and it comes with a unique set of problems that people have never faced before.

Thankfully, you no longer need to wader in the dark anymore, as many case studies and journals have been written about the subject. These resources can provide you with the answer you need for just about any parenting challenges.

From all of these scientific documentation comes a parenting style that has been proven to be very effective.

What is Positive Parenting

Before we discuss the definition of positive parenting, it helps to understand what a "parent" is. The first two things that may come to your mind are the father and mother. Many research focused on the role of the mother and how she is responsible for the initial stage of child development by providing nourishment and affection, whereas the father disciplines the child. This is a very traditionalist view. The roles are now mixed in recent days.

However, the point here is that the parents alone are not the only ones who influence the child's upbringing and their psychological wellbeing. There are others out there who function as caregivers such as adoptive parents, foster parents, siblings, etc. In other words, the term "parent' can apply to those people as well because their presence has an influence on their children's mental and physical wellbeing.

There are many definitions to positive parenting, but all of them agree that positive parenting is the continual relationship between the parent and the child that is characterized by the following:

- Caring
- Open communication
- Teaching
- Leading
- Providing
- Unconditional love

- Nurturing

- Empowering

- Consistency

- Affection

- Emotional security

- Emotional warmth

- Positive

Here, the positive parenting approach assumes that all children are born good and that they strive to do the right thing. It is only because of the misjudgment that caused them to do the wrong things instead.

Positive parenting also includes discipline that exists within the authoritative parenting style. Discipline here is structured in a way that builds a child's self-esteem and support open communication and mutual respect between the parent and the child.

The Research

The big question here again is whether positive parenting works and if you should go through the trouble of changing to this parenting style. There is actually much research that shows both short-term and long-term benefits of positive parenting on children's development. For a start, you have the Positive Parenting

Research Team (PPRT) from the University of Southern Mississippi, which has been involved in many studies aimed at studying the influence of positive parenting. They studied the relationship between positive parenting and academic performance, positive parenting as a predictor of protective behavioral strategies, and positive parenting on resilience, social support, and emotional health.

Other than that, Pettit, Bates, and Dodge conducted a seven-year study in which they studied the impact of supportive parenting on pre-kindergarteners. Supportive parenting here is similar to positive parenting in the sense that it emphasizes warmth, love, discipline, and positive involvement. This parenting approach is a stark contrast to a harsher parenting style.

Supportive parenting has also been shown to have led to better school adjustment and fewer behavioral problems as the child grows up. Plus, supportive parenting has the potential to even negate the impact of familial risk factors such as family stress, single parenthood, and socioeconomic disadvantages, among others.

At Gottman Institute, researchers have conducted their own investigation on the impact of positive parenting. They created a 5-step emotional coaching program that is designed to help children build confidence in themselves and promote healthy psychological and intellectual growth.

These five steps include emotional awareness, connection with the child, listening to the child, naming emotions, and finding solutions.

At the end of the study, Gottman reported that children who have received this emotional coaching have a more positive developmental trajectory compared to those that did not receive this coaching. Moreover, Bath Spa University conducted its own evaluation of emotional coaching and found the connection between the coaching and positive outcomes for families. For instance, parents report a 79% improvement in children's positive behaviors and wellbeing.

So, all the evidence suggests that positive parenting has a great impact on healthy child development. Positive parenting provides benefits that remain with the child well into adulthood.

Another way we can describe positive parenting is in terms of resilience, which we will discuss in a later chapter. When children have been raised with positivity for their entire life, even though they may be severely disadvantaged, they are more likely to thrive in the face of harsh circumstances.

Positive parenting is the way to go forward as it minimizes risk and providing the children with all they need to develop and thrive. Now we know that positive parenting works, let us look at exactly how it works.

How It Works

There are many ways that positive parenting influences and promotes a child's pro-social development. For instance, positive parenting has been shown to positively influence a child's temperament by improving their ability to regulate their own emotions. In fact, parental warmth and positivity from the parents play an important role in children's ability to regulate emotions. The mastery of this ability will lead to reduced externalizing problems when children grow up.

Other than emotion regulation, there are many other ways that positive parenting contributes to the child's development:

- Parental supervision promotes children's socializing skills

- Democratic parenting decision-making enhance relationships, self-esteem, and confidence in children

- Positive, open communication improve the child's problem-solving and social skills as well as enhancing the relationship

- Teaching and guidance help promote children's confidence

- Parenting methods that promote autonomy supports creativity and self-determination

- Providing clear boundaries and consequences teaches your children to have responsibility and accountability

- Supportive and optimistic parenting encourages children to have a more positive view of the future

- Providing recognition for desirable behaviors encourage your children to engage in healthy behaviors

In general, many aspects of positive parenting have been shown to improve the child's development in all areas in their life, including self-esteem, creativity, optimism, social skills, among others. Positive parenting provides the children with the love and warmth they need to nurture their spirit, which gives them the strength to approach life without fear.

Child's Age

Positive parenting is most effective when the children are young, under one-year-old if possible. However, that does not mean that positive parenting is ineffective when your child is any older. The key takeaway here is that you want to start positive parenting as soon as possible. Establishing a secure attachment between the children and their parent lead to many positive developmental outcomes such as trust, self-esteem, among others. Children are more susceptible to external influence when they are young, so it is a good idea to start practicing positive parenting as early as possible. A downside of positive parenting is that it takes a long time and requires consistency, so the time it takes to establish a solid parent-child attachment and positive behaviors and habits to be established in children are shorter the younger your children are.

This attachment is the foundation of positive parenting and should be prioritized early on. It is related to early positive developmental outcomes as well as other long-term psychological and behavioral benefits for the children.

Positive Parenting Styles

Positive parenting is characterized by the parents being warm yet firm with their children, and such parenting style has been linked to several positive outcomes among children. Another way to approach this parenting style is by being assertive, but not intrusive, demanding, but responsive. Other than a positive parenting style, the developmental parenting style has also been shown to yield similar results.

The developmental parenting style can be said to be another form of parenting style that is characterized by affection, responsiveness, encouragement, and teaching to support the child's cognitive development. This parenting style also happens to have many things in common with a positive parenting approach.

All in all, by studying positive parenting styles and strategies, you can implement them into your parenting methods to encourage healthy development for your children. Positive parenting is the best approach to raising children because it:

- Prioritizes positive family experience

- Acts as a positive role model

- Applies consistent and natural consequences for behaviors
- Rewards and encourage desirable behaviors
- Uses effective communication
- Pays attention to the child's needs and responds to those needs
- Attends to child's expressions
- Supports exploration and involvements
- Provides clear expectations and rules
- Provides enough monitoring and supervision

In short, positive parenting supports children's healthy development by being loving, firm, supportive, consistent, and involved. In order to accomplish this, you need to put in a lot of effort by communicating the expectations you have for your children as well as walking the talk by being positive role models themselves.

Positive Parenting, Toddlers, and Preschoolers

We all have to through this phase in our parenting adventure, and it is perhaps one of the most frightening things that anyone has to experience. It doesn't help if you hear jokes like "Having a two-year-old is like having a blender without a top."

Of course, handling toddlers and preschoolers is a nightmare. That much has been made clear. They seem perpetually drunk and will knock over everything they run into, not to mention that they make a lot of noise, experience constant mood swings, and has growing needs for independence. They're quite literally the small, feisty, and drunk version of yourself.

While it is adorable to see them stumbling and trying to communicate, they can frustrate you just as much.

Case Study

Let's put positive parenting into context and see how a parent should approach a troublesome child.

Bob is a father to 3 beautiful children, two sons, and a daughter. On one fateful weekend, Bob decided to take Jake grocery shopping. It was supposed to be a short trip, but boy was he wrong.

So, after fifteen minutes into their grocery shopping, they got everything they need, and they go to the cashier. Unfortunately, there is a long line there. They wait for 30 minutes before the son, Jake, had enough. Jake proceeds to throw each item out of the cart while screaming at the top of his lung.

Bob is visibly flustered as other people start to give him disapproving looks, whispering among themselves about his obnoxious child or how he sucks at parenting. Bob is just as frustrated about the situation as his son. At first, he tries to ask Jake to stop, perhaps by asking him nicely or trying to reason with him.

But it doesn't work. He proceeds to use other approaches, including commanding, pleading, threatening, negotiating, anything he can think of out of desperation. But Jake is out of control and cannot be reasoned with. Bob wants Jake to end his tantrums immediately. What Bob didn't realize is that all the quick fixes he can think of may actually have negative consequences in the long run, regardless of whether he succeeded in any of his attempts.

So, what should Bob do in this scenario?

Before we go to discuss specific solutions for his situation, it is crucial that we understand Jake's developmental stage. Jake does not throw tantrums for no reason. Why he does what he did is probably because it is something that is biologically programmed inside his brain to ensure his survival.

For instance, children between the age of 2 and 3 start to understand more and more about the world around them. Unfortunately, they are programmed to believe that the world is hostile and scary. Therefore, they can become anxious easily. Certain insignificant things such as bad weather, nightmare, stranger, strange images, the hospital or dentist, animals, etc.

Fear for such things is inconvenient for parents. They only make parenting more complex than it already is. However, they also serve as an indicator of maturity.

In this case, Jake here is reacting this way because he is anxious and wants to avoid potential danger. His reaction supports his positive development. Of course, while fears of superficial things like monsters do not reflect true danger to the child, they learn from their experience by avoiding individuals who appear to be mean or aggressive.

Similarly, fear of strangers is also a protective mechanism that encourages children to stay close to adults who they know can keep them healthy and safe. You want your children to be able to discern good people from bad without instructions, after all. While their sometimes irrational fear can be an annoyance for parents, it is better for children to be cautious and overestimate dangers because they are following their survival instincts by using false-positives. In this case, it is better to run away from a harmless situation than being caught in a dangerous one because of misjudgment.

Therefore, as a parent, you need to respect your children's fear, meaning that you do not punish them for feeling frightened. So, talk to your child in a calm and loving way and try to get them to verbalize their feelings. Therefore, you need to see the positive in the negative. In this case, your child throwing tantrums is an opportunity for you to understand and develop a stronger bond with your child.

With this goal in mind, any course of action that you may choose to approach a frightened or anxious child should always take the long-term goal into consideration (positive development). It can be hard to keep that in mind in the heat of the situation, but it will be worth it in the end.

On the other hand, punishing behaviors such as yelling will not help you in the long run. A way to help you calm down and try to sympathize with your child is by seeing them as a high school student or adult. Doing this can help you respond in a more reasonable way.

What are your long-term goals to keep in mind when dealing with troublesome children? They are:

- Maintaining a quality relationship
- Taking responsibility
- Being respectful
- Knowing right and wrong
- Making the right decisions
- Being honest

All of these are long-term goals that parents need to keep in mind and are highly relevant to our case here. If Bob only wants Jake to stop yelling and throwing tantrums, he would only be thinking about the short-term goal, which is to get Jake to cause a scene. Bob may promise to give Jake some candies if he stops. Suppose that Jake does stop and calms down, Bob can proceed to get out of the grocery store quickly and without suffering from humiliation anymore. He might even feel good about himself that he managed to calm Jake down.

This works as far as stopping Jack from causing a scene. This solution may solve the problem today, but there may be other unforeseen circumstances such as:

- Jake may throw tantrums again to get some more candies

- Jake may do every time they go shopping or going outside for that matter, and he will demand more candies

- Bob may never take Jake anywhere else ever again

- Plus, when Bob gave Jake candies to calm Jake down, the message Jake receives from the candy will not reinforce the qualities Bob want to see in his son in the future such as:

- Being respectful for others

- Being responsible

- Being considerate and courteous

- Being helpful

- Knowing right from wrong

- Having good social skills

- Having good manners

Therefore, what Bob should have done in this situation is for him to stay calm. Then, Bob can then tell Jake that he needs to stop, or he will get a time-out. In this case, a time-out means that Bob will take Jake somewhere where he cannot get reinforcement for his negative behaviors such as an audience. So they can either go to a quiet corner in the grocery store or head straight outside to sit in the car until Jake calms down.

If the store is very crowded that day, Bob can just ask the clerk to put his cart somewhere safe while Bob removes Jake from the scene. Bob can even ask the clerk to save his place in the line until he returns, which is not an impossible request if it means getting Jack to be quiet. After a quick time-out, Bob can give Jake a hug and let Jake know what he should do for the shopping trip as well as the consequences for breaking the rules.

If the situation is really extreme, it may be better for Bob if he just takes Jake and heads straight home, even if it means not doing the grocery. It is not ideal, but it is a small price to pay if it means getting Jake to learn how to behave.

Most importantly, if Bob does take Jake home, Bob needs to make sure that the trip back home is not rewarding for Jake. That means Jake cannot get home and go straight to watching TV, play video games, or doing anything that he enjoys. Bob needs to put Jake on a time-out immediately upon arrival. In this case, Bob can even tell Jake that he won't be eating his favorite meal tonight because the shopping was not done.

This is the natural consequence of Jake throwing a tantrum, which is not meant to be punitive or sarcastic. Here, Jake understands that if he causes a scene at the store again, he will not get to eat his favorite food. But that is still not enough. Bob, even though he may not feel like it, still need to talk to Jake in a kind and loving way.

This is the important bit. Whatever approach Bob chooses to address Jake's problem, he needs to stick with it. If he doesn't, Jake will get the impression that he may get something that he wants one day if he keeps acting up. It starts to create a pattern of reinforcement and a negative feedback loop. Once it begins, it will be very difficult to break.

Of course, that does not mean that Bob needs to take Jake out of the store and get no shopping done. That is just impossible because Jake has too much control. Therefore, Bob needs to plan ahead and make Jake aware of the rules and expectations of his behaviors, as well as the consequences of breaking the rules.

Here, Bob needs to be specific about the rules, expectations, and consequences. "I expect you to behave at the store," is just too vague. Instead, Bob needs to say something like, "The rules for shopping are that you need to be quiet, talk quietly, listen to me, and sit still in the cart." Another thing Bob can do is to determine whether he wants to take Jake out shopping in the first place. He can consider when to take Jake out when he is most likely to behave, such as when he well-rested, fed, and not upset.

Bob can also keep Jake busy by giving Jake something to do during the shopping trip. Jake can perhaps bring his favorite book along and read, or help put items in the cart. When Bob gives Jake options, Jake will feel a sense of control because he can choose between reading and helping out.

Finally, Jake should be rewarded if he behaves properly. Such a reward includes praises or other privileges. If Bob decides to praise Jake, he needs to be specific about it too. Another form of reward is experience. For instance, if Jake behaves and the shopping went smoothly, Bob can decide to reward his son by taking him to the park before heading home.

Bottom Line

Positive parenting is an effective approach to raising kids, although it requires a great deal of patience from the parents. There are a few more things you need to know about positive parenting:

- Seek help: Parents are never alone. Whatever problems you have with your children, you can always turn to other parents online for help. There are many communities of parents out there dedicated to helping parents solve their child-related problems.

- Start early: As mentioned previously, positive parenting is most effective when you start as early as possible. If you do it right, then the process from when your child is a toddler to a teenager should be relatively stress-free.

- Empower: The whole idea of positive parenting is to empower the child to be their best selves. Being positive parents is being warm, loving, caring, and so much more. In the end, children are able to reach their full potential as fulfilled and resilient individuals in society. To reach this level, you need to be consistent and clear about your expectations. Your children have to understand those expectations. The parents also need to know what their children are doing and try their best to encourage positive behaviors. This parenting style emphasizes making the environment at home positive and constructive. Being positive parents means that you need to love your children unconditionally, no matter who they are, and support their individuality and autonomy. This is only possible through open and honest conversation and being affectionate, empathetic, as well as supportive.

- Benefits: Positive parenting has been proven to have many benefits for the child's development, including self-esteem, externalization, decision-making skills, and social skills, among many others. All of these benefits are often permanent.

- Positive discipline: Positive discipline is a proven approach to discipline children in a kind and loving way. It does not result in emotional traumas in your children, as it is not permissive or punitive. It does not involve anger, yelling, or punishment. Instead, it is all about rules, expectations, consequences, and consistency. This is a long-term solution to your child's behavioral problems.

- Application: Positive parenting can be used widely, regardless of your family situation. It is applicable in many situations, even to some of the worst problems out there. For instance, it can be used to resolve temper tantrums, bedtime and eating problems, sibling rivalry, and many more.

- Flexibility: When it comes to positive parenting, there are many ways to approach a problem. You can find out more about them online as many studies have been done on various parenting problems, and experts have identified positive parenting solutions to all those problems, all of which are based on scientific evidence.

When you think about it, you already have access to a vast library of knowledge on positive parenting beyond this book. All that we have discussed here are just some of the fundamentals that you need to know. Even if you do not look for more, the information presented here is sufficient to help you discipline your children in a positive way. In the end, after you have consistently and patiently applying positive parenting strategies, you will establish a deep and meaningful connection with your children that will last a lifetime.

Chapter Three

Communication

As discussed in the previous chapter, one of the main elements of parenting style is communication. How you communicate with your children influences how they grow up. This is what we will discuss in this chapter.

Listening Skills

Believe it or not, but the biggest part of communication is listening skills. As a parent, it can be difficult to sit there and listen to your children ramble on and on. In many cases, you do not need to do much for them. Just be there for them and listen. Listening skills are not just about being able to receive verbal messages. It is also about being able to perceive the nonverbal cues from children. In fact, every one of us communicates nonverbally more than verbally. Listening is a learned skill, but you can become a better listener with practice. In addition to making your children feel included and cared about, you will set a good example for your children as they, too, will become good listeners.

In this case, you need to be an active listener. Doing so tells your children that they are free to share their opinions, thoughts, and emotions. There are many skills you can learn so you can be an effective listener. They all help you understand your children more, therefore strengthening the bond between you and your children. To become an active listener, you need to:

- Allocate: Set aside some time and listen to your children. That means paying all of your attention to what they have to say as well as choosing the best time and environment for the conversation. Pick a place with no distraction. As for the time, you need to experiment a bit. Some parents say that they communicate the best right before bedtime or during dinner.

- Listen: Put aside your own thoughts or perspective and just listen. Focus on what your children have to say by giving them all your attention. Try to understand them by putting yourself in their shoes. Make them feel that you care and understand what they think and feel.

- Reflect: After listening, repeat what your children said back to them in your own words. This is reflective listening. When appropriate, try to rephrase what they are saying in your own words and tell them what you think they are trying to say. Do not just say the exact same thing, which is parroting. Read between the lines and really see what they are trying to say based on their tone and body language. Remember that what your children say does not necessarily fully reflect what they feel, so you need to understand the entire message by reading the nonverbal cues. When you repeat the message, give the emotion a label. For instance, "It seems like you are upset about…"

- Eye contact: Show that you are paying attention by maintaining eye contact with them and nod your head, occasionally interjecting with responses like "I see," or "Oh," Doing so encourages your children to keep talking.
- Accept: Respect what your children are saying and accept it, even if it does not coincide with your own ideas and expectations. This is easy because you just need to listen and not criticize, judge, or interrupt them.
- Create: Give your children the opportunity to solve problems on their own. As a parent, your role is to guide and encourage them. Whenever they come to you with a problem, sit down and talk about it. Explore your options, and you should reach a solution that works for both you and your children.

Parents who are active listeners are described as having good intuition and tuned in to their children. Through the simple act of paying attention and seeking to understand your children, you can grasp how they think and feel about a particular matter. As an added benefit, your children are more receptive to your suggestions because they believe that you truly care about them and that whatever you suggest is for their own good.

In the end, your children will feel loved and connected. They will be able to cope and solve their own problems as well as control their behavior and emotions in the future.

Remember, being an active listener does not mean that you have to agree with everything the other person says. What makes you a good listener is the fact that you understand what the other person is trying to say. You do not need to agree with your child. In many cases, they just want to vent and get their frustrations out of their chest, so the best thing you can do for them is to listen.

There are many ways to determine whether you are listening actively. If you feel bored by the conversation, become distracted and look around or away, or feel rushed or feel that you are wasting time, and then you are not listening actively.

It is worth practicing active listening to your children now. For instance, whenever you are talking about anything, ask your children to repeat in their own words what you have been trying to say. Try to get them to understand the underlying message and your emotions behind your words. You also need to do the same.

Talking Techniques
When you talk to your children, try to make it positive by not imposing judgment or placing blame. That means using the word "I" instead of "you," especially when you are trying to change your children's behavior.

For instance, instead of saying, "You need to help out around the house," say, "I would like some help with the chores around the house because I'm tired after work." You are suggesting the same thing, which is asking your children to help with chores, but the latter is a lot gentler, and your children are more compelled to help you that way.

The "I" statement tells your children about the effect of their behavior on you. You can communicate the same thing using the "You" statement, but they are more threatening. Moreover, your children would be encouraged to take responsibility for their actions. Using the "I" statement also tells your children that their parents are willing to express their feelings and belief that their children will respond in a positive, responsible way.

On the other hand, "You" statements such as "You should not do that" emphasizes the child's action and place the blame on them, thus creating distance between you and your child. This also encourages them to put on a defense and counter-argue, discouraging effective communication.

Worse still is the "put-down" messages that criticize or judge children. They include name-calling, embarrassing, or ridiculing the child. Such messages can cause long-term and severe psychological damage to children, especially their self-esteem. If you say that your child is stupid, a disappointment, a failure, or anything along that line, they may continue to perceive themselves that way for the rest of their life.

The "I" messages are more positive overall because it highlights what you feel about your children's actions without placing the blame on them. This encourages them to be responsible and assume more responsible roles if they understand the situation and needs and feelings of others.

Of course, that does not mean that things will change for the better the moment you start using the "I" statements. Your children may not pay much attention to it at the start. If this is the case, continue using the statements. You can try to say it in a different way or with greater intensity. Sometimes, children do not really understand you, so you should be willing to say something like, "This is how I feel, and I do not appreciate being ignored."

However, if you have practiced active listening and proven yourself that you are receptive to your children's wants and needs, they should be more responsive to your own as well. Be patient and give them some time.

Another thing worth mentioning is that you should be very careful about your tone of voice. Make sure that it is consistent with your message. You will come off as insincere when you say one thing but sound the other.

Consistency is key here. If you have more than one child, then you must have the same communication approach and style with every one of them, even though you are free to alter your approach according to each child's temperament. Do not play favorites or appear to do so, or be more receptive to one child than another.

Improving Family Communications

In addition to being an active listener and using the "I" statements, there are many other things you can do to improve communication within the family:

Be Available

Allocate a certain time of the day to have a family talk. Just 10 minutes a day is enough as long as there are no distractions. During this time, encourage your children to talk about their day and what they think and feel about this. Ten minutes may seem small, but it makes a big difference as it helps your children learn good communication habits. So, turn off the radio and television. Pay full attention to your children as they speak. Maintain eye contact and seek to understand their feelings.

Remain Calm

There will come a time when you feel that your patience has run out. However, keep in mind that exploding on your children is not the way to go. There are other ways to help your children without hurting their feelings. Here are a few tips to help you calm yourself before you talk to your children:

- Slowly take a few deep breaths.
- Wait a few minutes before you talk to your child.
- Find a word to describe your emotion, say it to yourself, and determine whether it is appropriate for your child. You don't want to label your child negatively.

- Share your frustration or general feelings with your friend, other family members, or spouse.
- Never hold grudges. It's not worth it. You're better off using your energy to deal with the problem right now.
- If you feel that you have lost control, seek professional help.

Be a Good Role Model

Keep in mind that children learn by example. Therefore, you need to monitor what you say and how you say it whenever you are around your children. You can use this opportunity to teach your children about good communication practices as well. As mentioned previously, make sure that your tone and message conveyed are consistent. For instance, if you say "No, don't do that," while you are laughing, it can be confusing for your child. So, be clear of what you say and how you say it. If you pick your words to describe your feelings carefully, your child will learn to do just that.

Show Empathy

As previously mentioned, active listening involves tuning in to your child's emotions and letting them know that you understand them. If your child is upset or sad, a hug or pat on the back can do wonders for them because you let them know that you understand what they are feeling. Never tell your children what they think or feel. Instead, let them express their emotions on their own. Take what they say about their feelings seriously. Never downplay them by saying something like, "You'll understand when you're older," or "It's naïve to feel that way," Your child's feelings are definitely real, and you should take it seriously.

Dos and Don'ts of Communication

Do:

- Be truthful. Never lie to your kids.
- Praise your child whenever you can.
- Calmly express your feelings about their good and bad behaviors.
- Listen to what your child has to say.
- Walk the talk – be the role model.
- Give clear instructions using vocabulary appropriate for their age and make sure your child understands you fully.
- If you are upset, make sure your child understands that it is their behavior, that is the problem, not the child.

Don't:

- Lie or tell your kid half-truths.
- Blame or call your child names. Instead of saying, "You're an idiot," say, "I don't how you behave there."
- Yell or threaten your kids.
- Give vague or unclear instructions like, "You better behave while I'm gone."
- Give your kids the silent treatment whenever you feel strongly about their behavior. It confuses and frightens children, especially if you used to show them warmth and affection.

Communication beyond the Family

What your children learn from you about communication influences how they communicate in the family as well as how they interact with others. All the communication skills will help your kid to negotiate, solve problems, learn from others, praise, express feelings, insights, etc.

If done well, communication is a way you can convey love, acceptance, respect, and approval to your kids. For instance, praising your child is no longer saying, "Good job!" To praise properly, you need to understand how your kid thinks about himself and his behavior and know when and how you can share his pride. That way, you can deliver your praise when he is the most receptive. Communication is a two-way process, meaning that it is not about what you say but also about how you deliver the message. If you communicate well with your kids, your relationship with them will not only thrive, but you are helping them develop, grow, and live up to their capabilities as a person.

However, a lot of people perform poorly when they need to express their acceptance. Some may think that their children may not be motivated to work harder even if they are told that they are fine the way they are. In reality, children tend to work harder when they are no longer pressured to win their parents' approval. Therefore, do not constantly judge and criticize your children. Instead, let them know that you love and accept them just the way they are. As a result, they will start to develop higher self-esteem and perform better.

Therefore, make an effort to communicate your acceptance through both your words and actions. You need to say that your child did a great job and hug them or offer other similar gestures.

Many parents fail to communicate their acceptance toward their children, either nonverbally or verbally. They may:

- Order: Do as you're told or else!
- Lecture: When I was your age, I had to do twice as many chores.
- Preach: You must not do that again.
- Criticize: What's wrong with you? You did it wrong again!
- Ridicule: You looked silly back there.
- Belittle: Come on. Someone, your age should know better.

This does not help children grow and develop their self-esteem. Instead, try to be positive and accepting when you talk to your children by:

- Praising whenever you can and be specific about it: You did a great job solving that math problem on your own last night.
- Letting your child know how much you appreciate them as they are: I'm so proud just seeing you run in the track meet today.

Another way to show your acceptance is by not getting involved in certain activities. For instance, if you let your kid paint on his own without you offering him advice on what he should or should not do, this will tell him that he is doing just fine on his own. The same applies to listen. When your kid comes running toward you with trouble in tow, all you need to do sometimes is just listen without interjecting with your own thoughts or comments that may contradict his feelings.

Chapter Four

Children's Behavior

Before we can understand how we can change children's behaviors, we need to understand them first. Many parents struggle to determine whether their children behave normally as they are or have more serious behavioral problems. The line is blurred between the two, so you need to really observe your children tell the difference. The first thing you should notice early on is any deviation from their "normal" behavior in the past. Children tend to behave consistently as they grow up, so any change in their behavior is a good indicator. However, the problem is determining their "normal" behavior because uneven development can influence their social behaviors and intellectual growth. Moreover, context also plays a role in determining the normality of their behavior.

As you can see, there are many factors to consider when you try to determine whether your child has behavioral problems. It is important that you understand your child's development so you can interpret, adapt, or accept their behavior as well as your own.

Types of Behavior
To help you better understand your children's behaviors better, I suggest you categorize them into three groups:

- Wanted and approved: Such behaviors include doing chores, being polite, doing homework, etc. In this case, you should praise your children.

- Tolerated: Such behaviors include not doing chores, being self-centered, or other regressive behaviors. These are not sanctioned but only tolerated under certain situations such as during a time of illness or stress.

- Unwanted: Such behaviors include anything that is harmful to the physical, emotional, or social wellbeing of children, family members, and other people. They might disrupt children's development. They may even be illegal or forbidden by ethics, religion, or society. That means destructive behaviors, racism, prejudice, theft, smoking, substance abuse, among many others.

Response

First and foremost, remember that your response is guided by whether you determine the behavior as a problem. Most of the time, parents either overreact to a small change in children's behavior or ignore or downplay the problem altogether. They may also seek quick and easy solutions when the problem requires a more serious response. Such responses can lead to difficulties in solving the actual problem.

Another thing to keep in mind is that different families tolerate different behaviors. For instance, talking back is unacceptable in a family in which the parents are authoritarian, and the same action is tolerated in a family in which the parents are permissive. It all depends on the parents' own upbringing, meaning that the parenting style that they adopt is learned from their own parents. However, that does not mean that the parents will respond consistently to the same behavior. Sometimes, the same behavior is tolerated in private, but not in public because parents feel that other people are judging them based on their children's behavior.

Another factor that influences how the parents respond is their temperament, mood, and pressure they have to endure on a daily basis. Parents who are easygoing tend to tolerate a wide range of behavior and take a while to label a behavior as problematic. On the flip side, parents who are strict tolerate a much smaller range of behaviors and are quick to respond and discipline their children. While the parent's temperament is determined mainly by their upbringing, other factors change rapidly throughout the day.

In some cases, parents may choose not to respond when their children's behavior is complex and challenging. They may try to:

- Rationalize: It's not my fault they behave that way
- Despair: Why are my children like this? Why mine?
- Wish it would go away: Kids will stop doing that eventually
- Deny: It's not a problem.

- Hesitate: I'm not sure if I should do something about it. It might hurt their feelings.

- Avoid: I don't want to upset them.

- Fear: They won't love me if I discipline them.

If you are worried about how your child develops or if you are unsure how to deal with the problem, consider consulting a pediatrician. They can help you determine whether your child's behavior is normal behavior or a problematic one and suggest a solution.

Common Habits

While the cause remains unknown, certain behaviors are common among children as they tend to be soothing or calming for them. Interestingly, adults tend to display the same habits during the time of stress. This includes sucking on their fingers or small objects, pulling their earlobes, or fingering their hair. So, here are some of the most common habits among children that concern parents:

- Hair twirling
- Fingernail biting
- Head banging
- Body rocking
- Thumb sucking
- Masturbating

Certain self-comforting habits such as thumb-sucking start in infancy and fade away in middle childhood eventually. However, as your child develops, they will limit this habit to a certain time of the day, such as at bedtime or when they are upset. Oftentimes, such behavior is accompanied by other behaviors in their early years, like cuddling with their pillow.

As children grow into teens and adults, they have greater self-control and self-understanding. When that happens, most of their self-comforting behavior starts to really fade away. This usually happens when they are 6 to 8 years old. Another factor that influences how soon or late, they grow out of their habits is how much socializing they get. Socializing and peer pressure help regulate their habits and behavior.

However, the self-comforting behavior may still persist in a small number of children, to a more serious degree. For instance, some children who used to rock themselves back and forth may not curl into a fetal position and move so much that the bed shakes and hits the wall, causing a lot of noise, until they fall asleep. While such habits are alarming, it is worth pointing out that the motions help soothe or calm children and serves as a transition from wakefulness to sleep.

Frequency and Intensity
The frequency of intensity of such habits is unpredictable and often ebb and flow for no reason at all. Sometimes, children tend to exhibit this behavior to the point that it hurts. For instance, children

who have a habit of biting their fingernails often cause bleeding or pain. In this case, it is possible that the consequences of their habits can dissuade them from continuing to do it in the future. A habit with such a consequence often fades away with time.

Management vs. Punishment

If you notice that your children are doing any of the above and that you know that they do it for self-comfort, perhaps the best thing to do is ignore them. Most of the time, these annoying yet alarming habits disappear with time. The worst you could do is to call them out using harsh words, ridicule your children, or punish them. Doing so creates additional tension, which further encourages this self-soothing habit, making it worse. Punishment is never an effective way to curb any habits.

However, ignoring the problem altogether can be difficult for many parents. They can ignore their children, but that does not mean they are not annoyed or frustrated. If that is you, try your best not to make any comments and wait for the habit to fade.

Children often seek out your help or are willing to cooperate with you to help curb their self-soothing habit if that habit has an element of pain as a direct consequence, such as nail-biting.

To help your children overcome annoying habits, consider doing the following:

- Praise your children when you notice that they are not doing the behavior for a long time.

- Use agents to introduce additional direct consequence to the behavior. Consider using bitter-tasting compounds that you can place on your children's nails to prevent them from biting on their nails. That way, your children associate the consequence with their behavior and eventually stop doing it. While this approach is not very successful in most cases, it is simple and can be effective if your children cooperate. Before you start, make sure to consult your pharmacist to get safe and digestible agents.

- Positive reinforcement is the best way to change your children's behavior. Reward and accentuate the behaviors you want your children to have. Monitor and reward (not punish) your children's behavior.

Chapter Five

Positive Reinforcement

Children are not born and know from the get-go what they can and cannot do. It is up to the parents, teachers, and their peers to educate them about behaviors that are acceptable.

As with any form of training, both for humans and animals, the best way to discipline children is through positive reinforcement. Positive reinforcement amplifies good behavior and curbs bad ones through the lack of reward. One of the best things about this discipline method is the fact that it does not hurt the child's feelings as much compared to other disciplinary methods. Therefore, the risk of your child developing psychological traumas is very low.

Positive reinforcement allows you to tap into your child's unique strengths and draw attention to their interests and personality traits. This creates an opportunity for you to connect and communicate effectively as well as encouraging your child to be himself.

What is Positive Reinforcement?
Positive reinforcement is one of many approaches to parenting. The idea is to encourage a desirable behavior through the use of a reward system immediately after the occurrence. That way, the recipient of the reward (children in this case) is more likely to

repeat the same behavior in the future. Eventually, through repetition, the recipient of the reward will develop a habit, and the reward is no longer needed.

Positive reinforcement follows the same principle of positive psychology in human nature, which focuses on what is good. Similar to positive psychology, positive reinforcement does not represent a complete view of human psychology. That means one cannot rely on positive reinforcement along to alter a child's behavior. Alone, it is very ineffective. However, if you use it to complement your parenting style, you will see the results much quicker.

Positive reinforcement, therefore, can be used to encourage behaviors we want to see, such as your children doing the chores without complaining about it or to reward them for doing something net but positive, or to encourage them to continue doing something.

Effective Positive Reinforcement

If you want to incorporate positive reinforcement into your parenting methods, it is worth pointing out that you need to invest a lot of time into it for positive reinforcement to be effective. It might require you to alter your habit because it may be required if you want to change your children's behavior. Some parents have to make drastic changes to the way they behave themselves, but it is all for the benefit of their children and themselves. Some may have to develop a habit to praise instead of criticizing, but to praise well.

This may seem awkward the first few time, but with practice, time, and consistency, you will get there.

Many parents feel the urge to correct and fix behavioral problems. Such tendency means well, but it often takes us away from many opportunities to notice what our children already perform well in. We tend to over-rely on fixing the problem, which harms the child's self-esteem, instead of praising them for all the things they did right.

According to a study conducted by Barbara Fredrickson on positive emotions, positive emotions are five times more powerful than negative emotions when it comes to happiness level. This 5 to 1 ratio also applies to positive reinforcement compared to other forms of correcting behaviors such as positive punishment or negative reinforcement. Therefore, positive reinforcement should yield better results in children and leads to happier children and parents.

Using this model, we can see that the use of positive praise outweighs criticism 5 to 1 in terms of influence. It is not just about making the child happy, either. If you learn to praise instead of criticizing, you too will feel the positivity and be generally happier. This leads to a very positive environment within the family.

Growth, Development, and Self-Efficacy

In order to make your praise effective, you need to emphasize the action, not the person. Therefore, praise your child by saying what they did is good. Professor Carol Dweck of Stanford University explained how praising the effort put into the activity instead of the personality of the child encourages a growth mindset as well as a sense of self-efficacy.

In her book titled "Mindset: The New Psychology of Success," she stressed the importance of focusing on the things that the child can control, such as their ability to pursue goals or commitment to learning new skills. It is never worth it to shift your attention toward something that is inherent and cannot be changed, such as your kid's personality.

Affection is especially crucial in how you communicate your approval. Whatever the circumstance may be, the best way to encourage a change in a child's behavior is through the effective use of emotion communication. As a parent, it is up to you to express warmth and compassion in enhancing closeness between the parents and children. With this strong emotional connection, you can achieve anything.

Autonomy, Competence, and Relatedness
A good way to develop a sense of autonomy in children is by involving them in setting limits and offering them choices for rewards that they perceive is meaningful and enjoyable.

To do that, you need to know your children well, especially their interests, and understand their emotional world. This is not easy, but it is worth the effort because you can easily connect to your children emotionally.

A great way to start tuning into your child's pursuits is by being curious, even if it is something that you are not interested in. Set aside your judgment and be open-minded, at least until you know your kid well. Doing so is a great learning opportunity for both the parent and the child.

You can also reinforce your child's self-esteem or sense of competence by reinforcing the behaviors that speak to their strengths and be developed by creating opportunities for the mastery of skills and practice of perseverance and commitment. However, that does not mean that you should avoid letting your children fail altogether. Parents that are overprotective and employ a fail-avoidant parenting style will undermine competence, independence, and academic potential and can lead to a life of anxiety for children.

Of course, all parents want to protect their children. However, safe and overprotected children feel that they are incompetent. After all, why else would you go to such length to protect them? The best way to learn and grow is through mistakes and failure. That is how everyone does it, and so should your kids. They learn to be resourceful and innovative from their failures. It does require bravery from your children, but you can help them here by giving them lots of love and support. Failure is not that bad. It fosters grit, autonomy, and competence, and helps you as parents to learn to back off and see the bigger picture and teach your children to embrace the opportunity to fail.

Examples of Positive Reinforcement

The use of positive reinforcement can be found pretty much everywhere, from dog training to employee reward and negotiation programs. Positive reinforcement is often the most apparent in schools and childcare centers because they need to encourage children to perform a task, learn a new skill, or behave a certain way. You can do that at home as well.

Some examples of the use of positive reinforcement in schools or childcare centers include:

- Compliments

- Recognition

- Praise

- Positive notes

- Pats on back, claps, high-fives, handshakes, smile

- Being assigned as the teacher's helper

- The privilege of choosing chores

- The privilege of reading, playing, crafting, or other activity with someone

- Extra credit or points

- Having work featured on a place of honor

- Homework-free night

- The privilege of choosing which activity to partake in

- Time or lunch with someone special

- Increased recess time

As you can see, you can incorporate many of these rewards systems into your parenting methods. Children of all ages often respond well to praise because they want to make you happy and be seen as making good choices. Children are more likely to repeat a behavior when you praise them for it. So whenever you catch your child in the act of being good or even when they behave in a way that you like, make sure to let them know that you appreciate it.

For instance, you can tell your kid, "I like the way you're keeping all the pencils neatly in one place on your table." This encourages your child to be organized, and this compliment works better than when you criticize him when he accidentally knocks one over. It helps to be specific about your praise as it tells your child exactly what he did right.

If you must respond negatively to your children's undesirable behavior, make sure to make at least five positive comments before you give one negative response.

Children and teenagers want and need approval from their parents so you can use descriptive encouragement to motivate them to do better. If you notice your teenage child is behaving responsibly and making rational choices, be sure to praise them for it. However, keep in mind that teenagers prefer to be praised in private rather than in front of their friends.

For teenagers, the best form of reward is increased privilege or responsibility. To do that, you need to sit down and discuss the rules with your kids and adjust them as they grow. For instance, you can extend their curfew as they get older so long as they behave responsibly.

Using Positive Reinforcement to Encourage Behavioral Change

Before you start using positive reinforcement to change your child's behavior, keep in mind that it will take a long time. You need to have patience and perseverance. The only downside to positive reinforcement is that it takes the longest to yield results. When you use it to encourage your children to drop an old habit, it takes even longer. For such a task, you need to practice frequency and consistency.

Frequency and Consistency

Positive reinforcement relies on frequency and consistency for it to be effective. For this reason, it is highly recommended that you create a reward system to keep your children motivated and committed, especially when they are learning a new skill. There are three stages to the implementation of a positive reinforcement reward system.

The first form rewards the most frequently and consistently. Here, you need to reward your child every time they do something right.

It is not easy to maintain, but it is recommended that you do that at the early phase of learning because reinforcement at this stage is intense and effective.

From there, you can start to provide reinforcement at a fixed interval or occurrences after a short time. At this stage, your child should be familiar with the reward system, so you can discuss it with them. The idea is to introduce a reward system that does not require as much work as that in the previous stage while still being worthwhile for your kids.

Finally, you can introduce a variable schedule when you start to offer rewards less frequently as time goes on. This is done to reduce your child's dependence on the reward. Over-reliance on the reward means that your child would not perform the desired behavior unless you reward them, which is not desirable. You want your children to develop a habit of displaying desirable behavior even in the absence of reward.

It is important that you also monitor your children's progress and make adjustments to the reward system based on your child's preferences. If you understand their interests, you can change the rewards to cater to their needs better, therefore increasing the effectiveness of the reward and motivate them to behave well. Alternatively, you can also offer your child a choice in the rewards, which foster independence.

Keep in mind that children get used to the reward over time, so it loses its power the longer you use it. To prevent this, I recommend you switching things up to bring in variety. You can do this by changing how often your children receive the reward or change the reward altogether. Taking away the reward frequency is recommended as it helps your kids wean off on the need for rewards and start behaving in a desired way as a force of habit.

What Rewards Are Best?
Children need to be given a very good reason if you want them to behave in a certain way. They will not do something if you do not give them something worthwhile. However, there are situations in which the reward is the result of the behavior. In this case, you do not need to reward them anymore. There are four main forms of rewards:

Natural rewards are those that are the direct consequence of desirable behavior. This kind of reward creates a positive feedback loop. That means the result of the behavior encourages kids to continue doing it. Natural reward includes the satisfaction from the job or a good grade. If at all possible, I recommend you use this form of reward to encourage children to adopt a certain behavior because it gives children self-esteem, a sense of meaning, and motivation.

Another form of reward is social rewards. These are approval or recognition from peers in the form of praise, compliments, encouragement, etc. Humans are social animals and will actively seek out acceptance and try to cultivate a sense of belonging. Social rewards satisfy that need.

Tangible rewards are self-explanatory. They are the things you use to encourage children to behave in a certain way. For example, you offer your kids some candies if they can keep quiet for the car ride. The biggest mistake parents make when it comes to positive reinforcement is overusing tangible rewards. Again, strive to make natural rewards the only reward children get from behaving a certain way.

Token rewards are the final form and are used in place of tangible rewards but can be just as effective as the previous form. Children can use the token immediately to get a certain tangible reward or save it to track their progress toward a bigger goal. You can use token rewards as a visual representation of continuous effort. Here, you need to create a point-based reward system in which your children can trade their accumulated points in to get something of value to them. They accumulate points by displaying the desired behavior.

After the behavior is well-established, you want to take the reward away to reduce your children's reliance. To do that, you need to decrease the frequency of the reward or lengthen the intervals between the action and the reward. That way, you can start to disconnect the task from the reward.

Does it Work?
Many happy parents have reported having success with positive reinforcement. However, keep in mind that positive reinforcement is more than just rewarding your children whenever they do

something right. It is so much more than that, and you need to be aware of the caveats. Positive reinforcement forms a part of positive discipline, which is characterized by the lack of punishment. This disciplinary form ensures that children are protected from psychological or physical damage.

To discipline positively, you need to be kind yet firm. That means offering help and guidance wherever needed but giving your child enough autonomy to give them the opportunity to grow. There are seven core perceptions that you should foster in children:

- Interpersonal skills

- Intrapersonal skills

- Responsibility, integrity, adaptability, and flexibility

- Personal power

- Perception of one's importance

- Judgment and evaluation skills

- Sense of agency and personal capability

Benefits and Advantages

As the name suggests, the biggest benefit of positive reinforcement is positivity for both parents and children. You get to discipline your children successfully without being affected by the negativity. You learn to focus on the nice things in life, and your children are happy. Parents who discipline their children through violence tend to feel bad about it, and it does not foster a positive environment in the household.

For this reason, many parents agree that it is better for their own emotional health if they focus on the good thing instead of the bad ones. That is not to say that constructive feedback or honesty is not adjustment. However, you need to balance between discipline and praise.

Punishment of any form can cause long-term negative effects, and positive reinforcement seeks to prevent that. More often than not, the damage of punishments is unseen until it is too late. It leads to resentment, distrust, rebellion, or even revenge. Punishment does not solve the problem as it encourages the kids to learn to avoid it. That means cheating, lying, or being defiant. They may not listen to you anymore because they think that you do not have their best interest at heart. Worse still, they may internalize your blaming and punishment and become the person you say they are: idiot, dummy, etc.

Punishment can take the form of grounding or outright violence, which is pretty common in Asian countries. Punishment does not have to go that far. Positive reinforcements have their own form of punishment, which is the lack of reward. You can deal with problematic behaviors in children through communication and emotional connection. If your parent-child bond is strong, then you can help your child learn from their mistakes without causing emotional traumas.

What has been said so far all points to the application of emotional intelligence, which is important everywhere from professional to personal relationships. It is the key to effective parenting. Having a high level of emotional intelligence takes a lot of practice on your part, but it is beneficial for both you and your children if you start learning and practicing it right now. Start right now, and be a role model for your children. Teach them how to cope with negative emotions and foster deep, meaningful relationships with you and their peers. Here are some suggestions:

- Be a role model
- Be precise in your speech
- Apologize if you are wrong
- Respect your children's needs
- Don't downplay their emotions
- Help your children solve problems.

What are the Drawbacks?
A quick look at positive reinforcement can tell you that it is hardly any different from bribery. However, there is a major difference. Both of them encourage children to behave in a certain way, but the result is different. For bribery, children only do something when

you give them rewards before they do it. This creates a reliance on the reward, which is something positive reinforcement avoids.

As flawless as positive reinforcement may seem, there is one thing you need to watch out for overuse. Positive reinforcement relies on the reward system to encourage children to behave, but it is not effective if you overuse it. This blunts the effectiveness and can lead to many more problems in children.

Praising your children too much can give them the illusion that they are a much greater person than they actually are. This false perception will be crushed immediately the moment they are exposed to any form of challenge, let alone failure. This can lead to long-term psychological traumas. You also need your children to develop resilience to be confident, competent, and content. This is only possible if you give them the opportunity to face hardships on their own and overcome them to build self-confidence.

As mentioned before, children can become over-reliant on rewards if you overuse it. Therefore, make sure to praise sparingly. Make sure that each praise you give to your child is effective. Too much praising tells your child that you are not genuine, not to mention tiring for you. If not that, then you run the risk of reinforcing the wrong behavior.

How to Use Positive Reinforcement
Before you begin, it is worth considering your child's development stage because you need to consider what children cannot do and will not do. Younger children do not have the cognitive ability to

understand complicated reasoning and logic, so you need to set a realistic expectation when you use positive reinforcement with children. Also, plan for the inevitable and total meltdown in children as it is quite common among very young children and toddlers.

For toddlers, aggression is a common occurrence and is a part of their development. Aggression often stems from the lack of language skills, frustration, exhaustion, hunger, and the desire to be independent, a change in routine, or even boredom!

For young children, they tend to act out when they need your attention. You can use this to shape your children's behavior effective early on because they will do many things just to get your attention. It is a gift in itself. As mentioned before, you need to notice what your children are doing and praise them by letting them know about what they are doing and letting them know that you are happy about it. You can do so through the use of praise, encouragement, physical affection or gestures, or active listening. This is called positive attention.

Positive attention is most effective when you use it often. Doing so reminds your kid frequently about what you want to see repeated more often. Praising good behavior is effective when your child is learning a new skill or having trouble learning one. At the very least, you can praise your child's effort and instances of success. The best thing about positive attention is that you can give it anywhere and anytime. It is a form of natural reward that is beneficial for your children, and it teaches you to look for the positives.

Through the clever use of the reward system, you can assign your kid different responsibilities by making it a game and that the reward is some sort of privilege. Counting, sorting, and preparing snacks can be fun. Just make sure to follow it up with praise and encouragement to positively reinforce the behavior.

Practice active listening, which we have discussed in a previous chapter. Nod when your child talks or do anything that signals to them that you are listening to make them feel comforted and respected. Doing so helps them cope with frustration and tension, both of which can lead to undesirable behavior and help diffuse temper tantrums.

The most important thing when you practice positive reinforcement is to be firm. You need to be firm when you discipline your children, which is easier said than done. Your children may whine, and you may be tempted to give in. It is hard to resist, but you need to remain firm. If you fail to do so, you will end up reinforcing the wrong behavior and train your children to whine more.

Managing Undesirable Behavior

The best thing about positive reinforcement for children is the fact that redirection is still an effective way to manage undesirable behavior. If your child is misbehaving, then you can curb that behavior by turning their attention to something else that is positive that they can do to distract them. This works well if you can identify the trigger that causes undesirable behaviors in children.

The key to managing undesirable behavior is by identifying the trigger that causes it in the first place. You can easily identify that through a quick observation. If your children frequently fight over a toy, take the toy away. For this particular problem, you can use this opportunity to teach your children to share, which is also an important social skill that children should learn early on.

Planning Ahead

Prepare for the inevitable challenging situations. Make sure to plan in advance around your child's needs. If you want your children to change activities, tell them at least 5 minutes in advance. It can do wonders because you are giving them time to prepare for the next activity.

When tantrums strike and nothing you do helps the situation, then you may need to remove your child from the situation to give them a break. Think of it as a relaxation break rather than a time-out.

Finally, make sure to incorporate humor into the mix. It may just be the difference between a tedious chore and a fun activity.

Positive Reinforcement Techniques and Ideas

There are a few things you need to keep in mind when you use positive reinforcement. These tips can help you enhance the effectiveness of such reinforcement.

Environment

Create an environment that fosters good behavior. The environment around the child plays a role in shaping their behavior, so you need to arrange it in a predictable way to help them behave properly. Make sure that their space is safe, organized, easy to traverse, and filled with fun things to play and engage with. For older children, give them a quiet space with natural light dedicated to schoolwork if possible.

Structure and Limits

It is important that you set some house rules. Make sure that your children understand them and that the rules themselves are reasonable. You also need to adjust them as your child grows older. When it comes to communicating limits, spare no expense. Use all means to communicate the limits and try to emphasize them constantly verbally or through the use of visual reminders.

Children like to have a structure to follow, so try to stick to the schedule as much as you can. That way, your kids know what to expect next. For older children, try to get them involved in setting family rules. It is a democratic way to do things, and you want to make sure that your kids feel that their opinions matter. Try to set the rules in a way that empowers your children to participate in the running of the household actively.

Natural Consequences

Children learn pretty early on that their choices and action have consequences. They may get upset if they do not like these natural consequences, but they will only understand them if they have first-hand experience. For instance, if your child is responsible for packing her gear for a sleepover and forgets his favorite pillow, he will have to manage without it.

In many cases, the natural consequence is enough to dissuade children from negative behaviors or reinforce positive ones. However, there may be a time when you need to help them choose a positive alternative behavior, solve their problems, or find ways to prevent them from feeling helpless. In some cases, you may need to talk to your children about the natural consequence of certain behavior that you do not tolerate and make sure they understand and agree with it. After that, make sure you follow it up firmly, calmly, and consistently.

Be a Role Model
As mentioned previously, children learn by example. So be the kind of person that you want your children to be. It is important that you send a positive message to your children and be a good role model for them. They will watch you for clues on how to behave. If you do not practice what you preach, they will do as you do, not as you say. For example, if you want to teach your kids to be calm in stressful situations, you need to be calm in front of your children.

Learn to Live with Mistakes
House rules are important because they serve as guides to what your kids can and cannot do. However, you also need to evaluate the opportunity for conflict and negative emotions that can come

with the violation of those rules and whether the consequences really matter. While rules are important, you may need to think about rewriting them if you spend all of your time correcting, instructing, and saying no.

Most importantly, if you break the rule yourself, apologize to your children. I mean it. It teaches them to be brave and take responsibility and helps with the relationship. The house rules should apply to everyone under the roof, after all.

Consider Personality
Positive reinforcement works for many children, but that does not mean the same reward system works for everyone. Every child is different, so you may need to alter your intervention method based on their interests. Playtime as a reward may work for your eldest son, but your daughter prefers relaxation breaks.

Be Open-Minded
Be ready to have a discussion with your children and be open-minded. If your kid comes to you and tells you that her classmates do not like her, do not deny her feelings and say something like, "Don't be silly. They love you!" As mentioned previously, what your child feels is real, and a response like that shuts down the discussion completely, leaving no room for discussion and making your child feels unappreciated. A better approach would be to ask questions so you can understand your child and the situation better. Ask something like, "What makes you think that way?"

Try to understand your child's situation and work with him or her to find solutions. But before you do, allow your child the opportunity to exercise control and decision-making by asking for their ideas first. Encourage your kids to solve problems on their own because they will have to do that in the future. As a parent, your duty is to help your kid figure things out by offering guidance and encouragement. Only offer your opinions when asked.

Talk About Your Feelings

Try to have this conversation as often to familiarize your children with externalizing their feelings. You can do that by being a role model and talk about how you feel and how your child's behaviors affect you. Doing so helps them see things from your own perspective without placing the blame on them. This conversation is crucial as it helps you and your child understand each other better. As mentioned before, use the "I" statement when you talk about your feelings, describe the behavior as you see it (not the person), and request what you want them to do instead. If possible, try to involve older children to help come up with solutions.

Walk the Talk

Follow through with your promises, whether you like it or not. This helps foster trust and create mutual respect. Your children will learn that they can rely on you and that you will not let them down when you promise them something. They will also learn not to try to convince you to change your mind when you told them about the consequences of their breaking the rules.

When your children experience the consequences of their actions, do not interject. They will learn to disassociate you from the discipline.

Delegate Responsibility

Introduce your children to responsibility early on by giving them chores or things they can to do help out in the house. Give them lots of practice so that they can get better at it and praise them for building up their self-esteem. They need to do the chores around the house in the future anyway, so you might as well give them the training they need from now.

Reframe

In positive reinforcement, you need to focus on the positive. So, try to reframe your requests to be more positive. Instead of telling your kids what you don't want them to do, tell them what you want them to do instead. For instance, tell your kids to go outside and play football is much better than telling them to stop playing video games. The same goes for rules. Positive rules are better than negative ones because they guide your kids' behaviors in a positive way.

Positive Reinforcement Words

Other than what we have described above, you need to cultivate a positive environment in the household by using words that support positive reinforcements. These words I am about to show you can be used in many casual situations. Remember, positive reinforcement (and praise) is only effective when you say it as you mean it. Make sure your body tells your children that you really mean what you say.

- I'm impressed that you managed to stay quiet while you're doing your homework as I was finishing that paperwork, as I asked.

- I knew that you could figure out how to solve this problem by yourself. Good job!

- I like how you show respect in the way you spoke to your teacher this morning.

- Your turn to play is coming. I'm proud to see you being so patient.

- Thank you for coming home on time.

- I'm impressed that you decided to clean your room without me, even asking! Tell you what, we'll go to Taco Bell after school today as a reward for your hard work.

- I like the color that you pick for the dog's clothes

- I was worried that you would stay out longer than you said you would. I'm happy that you return on time.

Teenagers require a slightly different approach to positive reinforcement, as we have mentioned previously. Other than praising them in private rather than in public, you have a much more comprehensive approach. Here, you can use the appreciative inquiry process to encourage your teen to reflect. The appreciative inquiry follows a few core principles. They encourage teenagers to appreciate the present, imagine the ideal, and taking action right now.

The whole idea behind these core principles is to encourage teenagers to be optimistic about their current situation, be clear and precise about their goals, and take action to get them closer to those goals. The appreciative inquiry process keeps us on track by asking from us three things: AIA – Appreciate, Imagine, and Act:

- Appreciate

- Do you feel good about this situation?

- If no, are you focusing only on what you don't want from this situation?

- How can you change your view in a way to see more of the positive side of the things you want from this situation?

- Imagine:

- Are you precise about what you want?

- Are you giving your attention to what you want?

- If you do not feel good or content, are you focusing on what you want?

- Act:

- Do your actions and thoughts consistent with your desires?

- Is what you're doing, saying, and thinking align with what you want?

- If no, what can you do to help you get closer to your goal?

Phrases to Avoid

As mentioned previously, children are very receptive to the words you say. If you call them nasty names, they may internalize those names and become the very person you call them. With that said, here are a few phrases you should avoid:

1. "Not now, I'm busy." This is implying that whatever they have to say or show to you is not important. At least, not any more important than what you are doing right now. If you develop a pattern of ignoring your children when they are small, they will get the message that you are not interested in what they have to say. This can lead to problems in the future because they will be less likely to share as they get older, and the lack of communication will make it very difficult for parents. Moreover, children are more likely to pick up bad habits when they see that their parents leave them to their own devices.

2. "Why are you so mean to your sibling?" - This is an act of labeling, which is something that you should avoid at all

costs. Parents send very powerful messages to them by labeling them. When they are young, children tend to believe what they hear, even if it is something negative about themselves. They do not question the label. They just accept them and may even become a self-fulfilling prophecy. Your child may start to think of themselves that way, therefore undermining their confidence. In fact, even labels that seem to be neutral or positive can limit or place unnecessary expectations on them. For instance, the label smart means that you expect your child to perform well at school, while the label shy limits their social performance. Therefore, you should instead address specific behavior and leave the label (adjective) about your child's personality out of it.

3. "Don't be upset." - Keep in mind that all feelings are valid. While our parental instinct demands that we protect our children from feeling any negative emotions, you should not deny them those feelings. In reality, there is no wrong way to feel in any situation. We see things differently, after all. Therefore, you should instead validate their feelings.

4. "Why can't you be more like your sibling?" - One of the worst things you can do to your children is comparing them to their sibling or someone else. This implies that you wish your child is someone different. This can also lead to resentment between the child, you, and whoever you compare them to. It is easy to see why parents would do

this. We all need some sort of a frame of reference for our children's behavior or milestones. However, making comparisons this way does not encourage children to change their behavior. Instead, it will only undermine their confidence.

5. "You should know better!" - Keep in mind that learning can be a process of trial and error. This is especially true for children who just started to explore the world around them. They do not really know better than that. Therefore, when you use phrases like this, you undermine their willingness to learn and try out new things. This is neither supportive nor productive for the child's growth. So, cut your child some slack and give them the benefit of the doubt. Instead of blaming them, help them learn from their mistakes to prevent similar problems from occurring in the future.

6. "If you do that one more time, you'll be in big trouble." - This is threatening your child, which is wrong on so many levels. Threats are not a way to encourage change in children. The younger your child is, the longer it will take for them to understand. Many studies have shown that no matter what discipline method you use, children around the age of two years old are 80% more likely to commit the same mistakes again in the same day. Therefore, instead of threatening your children with punishment, you need to develop a repertoire of positive strategies such as

redirection, usage of natural consequences, or removal of the child from the problem.

7. "Wait till daddy/mommy gets home!" - This is an extension of the threats of punishment we have discussed previously. When you disconnect the punishment from the children's actions, its effect is minimal. For it to be effective, you need to address the situation immediately. If you delay the punishment or shift the responsibility of punishment to another person, it undermines your authority.

8. "Hurry up!" - Consider your tone when you talk to children, especially when you ask your child to hurry up. Children tend to feel guilty for slowing their parents down. Imploring your children to hurry up makes them feel bad, but does not make them move any faster. Instead, look for calm ways to speed things along.

9. "Good boy!" - Giving praise is a good thing, but vague praises are ineffective. When your compliments are indiscriminate, children tend to be confused. They do not know exactly what it is that warranted your praise. Moreover, they also know the difference between praise for when they did something that requires real effort, which is more satisfying and praise for something simple. For maximum effect, only praise your children for the things that require real effort and make sure you're specific with your praise, and praise the behavior (not the child).

Bottom Line

Family relationships are a major part of our lives as they often offer some of the most meaningful and intense experiences of how a family function as a whole can bring the children joy, a sense of belonging, acceptance, trust, and love, or none of it. It is in our best interest to focus on what you can do to bring the best out of your children, even though it is going to be a difficult task. Parenting is a huge responsibility, and it is filled with lots of frustration, anxiety, and sleepless nights.

Keep in mind that what you pay attention to can nurture or ruin the world you are constructing for yourself and your children.

Children born into this world need to know that their parents have certain levels of expectation from them and that whatever they do have consequences. At the same time, they know so little at their early age that you cannot expect them to know what to do in any given circumstances. Therefore, you also need to communicate the fact that you still love and accept them no matter who they are, no matter what happens. In a world where nothing is certain, they can at least be certain that you are there for them when they need emotional support.

The Michelangelo Phenomenon points out how we are shaped by the people around us, especially those who are closest to us. After all, birds of a feather flock together. For your children, you are closest to them. Therefore, you have the greatest influence on their personalities and potential. So, the burden rests on you to help your child shape their ideal self by affirming their potential, encouraging them to express valuable personality traits, as well as creating an environment that your child can feel safe in.

Chapter Six

Positive Discipline

When people mention the word "discipline," it seems to imply having a negative consequence. In reality, the word itself is defined as training that molds, corrects, or perfects the mental faculties or moral character. When you phrase the definition this way, discipline does not sound so bad. In fact, discipline is absolutely necessary for all of us.

The definition itself instructs us not to be tyrants, but as teachers. Because we are responsible for teaching our children, we need to make sure that we teach our children all the right things. Positive discipline is another element of the authoritative parenting style or positive parenting style. Positive discipline is not aggressive, violent, or critical.

Physical punishment, such as spanking, is never an answer. It does not encourage behavioral change in children and will only serve to cause resentment, which further undermines the parent-child attachment that is already fragile in the first place. Plus, such punishment can even cause emotional traumas in your children. Punishment is never the answer.

There are four main negative consequences of physical punishment, which are the 4Rs:

- Resentment: Your children will hate you and not trust you

- Revenge: Your children will find ways to get back at you for what you've done to them:

- Rebellion: Your children will not listen and do all the things you don't want them to do

- Retreat: Your children will simply run away to escape from your control

- There are five main criteria for positive discipline that you need to embrace if you wish to be effective parents:

- Kind but firm

- Promote children's sense of belonging and significance

- Long-term benefits

- Teach valuable life lessons and skills

- Help children develop confidence

Other than that, there are many key aspects of positive discipline, among those are empathy, self-respect, non-violent, respectful, and more. In other words, positive discipline is all about a mutual respect. It tells your children that no matter how poor, small, powerless, or vulnerable a person is, that person deserves to at least be treated as a human being, which is a very powerful lesson that the world needs to learn.

So now that we understand that positive discipline does not involve the use of punishment, what exactly does it involve? It involves the following:

- Mutual respect principle: Treating your child the way you want to be treated yourself

- Big deal principle: Using positive reinforcement in the right way to encourage and reward desirable behaviors

- Alternative principle: Give your child an alternative, desired behavior to replace the undesirable one.

- Choice principle: When you replace bad behavior with a positive one, give your child at least two choices to which positive behaviors they want. This gives them a sense of empowerment.

- Abuse it/lose it principle: Make sure that you take away the reward the moment your child breaks the rule.

- Connect before correct principle: Seek to understand your children first by making them feel loved and cared for before you attempt to address their behavioral problems.

- Validation principle: Validate the child's feelings. Always.

- Good head on your shoulders principle: Make sure to praise your children along this line whenever applicable. That way, you encourage them to feel capable, empowered, and in control. This is particularly effective for teenagers.

- Belonging and significance: Make sure your children feel important, appreciated, and that they belong.

- Timer says principle: To help your children establish a firm routine early on, it pays to have a timer to help them make transitions from one activity to the other.

Positive parenting is one of the four approaches parents take to modify their children's behavior based on the theory of operant conditioning. All of these four methods rely on two elements:

- Whether you are trying to encourage (reinforce) or discourage (punish) certain behaviors

- Whether you are adding a reward to encourage (positive) or taking away a reward (negative) from said behaviors

- The four types of behavior-modifying approaches are:

- Positive punishment, which adds something unpleasant to discourage behaviors

- Positive reinforcement, which adds something pleasant to encourage behaviors

- Negative reinforcement, which takes away something unpleasant to encourage behaviors

- Negative punishment, which takes away something pleasant to discourage behaviors

Initially, it is difficult to grasp these concepts because the term "positive" and "negative" does not necessarily imply that something is good or bad.

Operant Conditioning Theory
To understand exactly how positive parenting is effective, we also need to understand the operant conditioning theory. It has been applied to animal training and human development alike.

Behaviorist B. F. Skinner developed this theory of operant conditioning, and his work is worth a look if you are interested. In short, this theory is built on the reward and punishment system. When we tend to engage in behavior that rewards us and ceases doing so when it punishes us. We associate our actions with immediate consequences. This is how humans in ancient times learn what is good and bad – through trials and errors. When we are encouraged and rewarded for something that we do, that behavior is reinforced. On the flip side, when we are punished for it, we tend to avoid doing it again.

Now, let us examine the difference between positive punishment and negative reinforcement, as well as positive reinforcement and negative punishment.

Positive Punishment and Negative Reinforcement

Here, positive reinforcement strives to encourage change in behavior by adding something unpleasant, therefore pushing the children to cease engaging in certain behaviors. Meanwhile, negative reinforcement encourages behavioral change by taking away something unpleasant, therefore encouraging a behavior.

The difference between the two is that positive punishment seeks to discourage bad behavior by making it unpleasant for the child, whereas negative reinforcement seeks to encourage good behavior by taking away the unpleasant element of said behavior.

For example, positive punishment means spanking your child when she throws a tantrum. Here, you discourage her negative behavior by bringing the pain as a direct consequence. On the flip side, negative reinforcement means removing restrictions on your daughter when she follows the house rule. In this case, you encourage her to follow the rules by taking away some of them when she does.

Positive Punishment and Positive Reinforcement

The only difference between positive punishment and positive reinforcement is whether you want to encourage or discourage behavior. Both of these approaches attempt to alter behaviors by adding a direct consequence to the behavior, which can be something pleasant to encourage behavior (positive reinforcement) or something unpleasant to discourage one (positive punishment).

For instance, positive reinforcement is taking your son to Pizza Hut when he stays quiet when you take him to school. Here, his being quiet along the way is reinforced because you add something pleasant, which is taking him to Pizza Hut. That way, your son will understand that he will get pizzas if he behaves. So he is more likely to behave in the future.

Positive Punishment in Practice

There are many ways to use positive punishment to encourage behavioral change. They include:

- Yelling

- Forcing children to do unpleasant tasks

- Adding chores and responsibilities

- Implementing more rules

Of course, all of these punishments are not really good ways to discourage behaviors, especially for children. These are some of the things you need to avoid doing to your children.

Negative Reinforcement in Practice

So, what does negative reinforcement look like in practice?

- Letting your child have a day off from chores

- Extending curfew

- Giving more time on the TV

- Removing some house rules

Effects of Positive Punishment

While punishment sounds negative, it does not have to be. In operant conditioning, punishment is only a means to discourage a behavior. Punishment can be something as light as sitting your child down and explaining to him why he should not do that.

Positive outcomes from positive punishments include:

- Your child is informed that whatever he did is not tolerated and understands that he should not do it in the future

- Your child is given a punishment or has to suffer a negative consequence, which tells him that his behavior has consequences and will hopefully discourage him from doing it again in the future

- Your child has a good reason to behave properly in the future

- There are also a few downsides to consider when using positive punishment:

- Punished behavior is only suppressed, which means that it may return in the future if the punishment is no longer there

- It might make the child aggressive because it may lead the child to believe that aggression is the way to solve problems. This will happen for certain types of punishment, of course.

- It can create fear that can apply to other situations. For instance, if a child is punished for being disruptive, they may start to fear social situations.

- It doesn't necessarily encourage children to behave in a desirable way. It simply tells your kid what not to do, so you need to tell your child what they should do.

To maximize the effectiveness of positive punishment, you also need to throw in positive reinforcement in equal measure. That way, you have a healthy mix of rewards for good behavior and punishment for bad ones. Both positive reinforcement and positive punishments are necessary for positive parenting.

For instance, positive reinforcement encourages good behavior but does not tell what the child should not do. This is where positive punishment comes in. It tells the child what not to do, but its weakness is that it doesn't tell him or her what to do, but this gap has already been filled if you also practice positive reinforcement. These two methods complement each other perfectly.

Whatever flaws are left between these two are often mitigated when you practice both positive reinforcement and positive punishment, as well as communicate clearly what you expect to see from your children.

Using Positive Punishment

The best thing about positive punishment is that you can still discipline your child without getting physical, which we have already discussed above. There are many ways to implement positive punishment:

- Make consequences black and white: Make it clear that a behavior has a direct consequence, no matter the reason behind the behavior of how your children feel about the consequence. If they do it, they have to face the consequences. No questions asked.

- Use meaningful consequences: The consequence needs to be unpleasant enough, and it should also be associated with the behavior as well as the lesson you want your children to learn from it.

- Talk: Depending on the violation, talking alone is a punishment in and of itself. But you can use it in addition to punishment to try to understand the situation better.

- Do not get into an argument: Children may throw tantrums, and teenagers may act apathetically to your punishment. Whatever the case may be, do not feel tempted to get into an argument with them over the punishment. Be firm in your punishment.

- Engage in your child's interest: Ask your children some questions such as "What will you do so you won't get into trouble like this next time?" Because children want to avoid punishment, it helps if you prompt them to think of how they can behave better not to get punished again.

- Hold your child accountable: Make sure that you hold your child accountable for his behavior, whether he cares about the punishment or not. What is important here is their behavior, not their emotions or how much they care about the punishment.

- Do not show disgust, disdain, or sarcasm: The entire point of positive punishment is to teach your child how to stop behaving badly, not to demean them.

Another thing worth keeping in mind when you practice positive punishment is that there are limits to it. For instance, if you ground your children, they will only do their time, but it does not show them how to do better next time. Worse still, children who are frequently grounded eventually get used to it after they have developed ways to cope with the punishment, but they may still not understand and learn what you want to teach them.

Therefore, grounding is not necessarily a good punishment. Instead, tell your children what they should do next time. Grounding only restricts what they can and cannot do. Plus, it doesn't give children a choice about whether to behave properly or not. In fact, grounding may feel so restrictive that it does not give children an opportunity to learn from their mistakes and make better decisions, therefore not promoting growth.

Positive punishment only weakens behaviors, as mentioned previously. It does not necessarily mean that children will stop behaving improperly forever. In some cases, if a child fears being punished, they may instead behave badly when you are not looking instead of dropping the bad behavior and learning positive behaviors. They will behave properly when you can see them, but that is only because they do not like to be punished. This is why you need to practice positive punishment with positive reinforcement.

Bottom Line

Depending on how you apply positive punishment, it can be very effective or not effective at all. It depends on whether the punishment is proportionate to the seriousness of the behavior. With this, you can effectively discourage behaviors in children. If done incorrectly, your children will miss the point entirely and can even lead to mental health problems.

With a little common sense and the information in this section, you should have no problem implementing positive reinforcement in your parenting methods to encourage good behavior.

Chapter Seven

Developing Resilience in Children

Everyone has heard the term "that which doesn't kill you makes you stronger." In reality, while it does not kill most of us, many of us feel dead on the inside when adversary befalls them. Some unfortunate few turned toward a more permanent solution to a temporary problem.

Whereas others crumble, some people managed to weather the storm and come out of it all with a bright smile. Even though their life is crumbling all around them, they can still smile and go about their day.

Just what is it that protects these people from emotional traumas in our lives? This is exactly what positive psychology seeks to understand. This protective armor is called "resilience."

The reality is that there will come a day when we as parents are no longer able to protect our children from the harsh reality of life. They need to move out and live on their own. They have a whole life ahead of them. As harsh as it may seem, but children will never grow and become adults if we keep protecting them from all sorts of harm. For these reasons, it is best to teach our children how to be resilient.

The thing about resilience is that the sooner you start, the better. Think of children as a blank canvas. You can shape an image onto the canvas very easily when it is blank. Just like the canvas, children are more amenable to change because their personalities and brains are still developing. Moreover, they are also more vulnerable to stressors. Therefore, now is the best time to start developing their resilience to withstand emotional traumas and potentially prevent negative outcomes.

In this chapter, I will show you exactly why resilience is important in children and how you can develop that in your own children.

What is Resilience? Why is it so important?
Resilience describes a survivor more than a victor because of the fact that it is a person's capacity to overcome challenging or even threatening circumstances. A resilient individual is not invulnerable to emotional pain and suffering. They are just as vulnerable, except that they persevere and make it through.

Resilience is not a superpower, nor is it automatic or inherited. It is a learned behavior that becomes internalized and comes into effect when the person becomes stressed. Resilience allows your children to maintain control and push through challenges in their lives.

As with anything psychological, resilience is not just one skill. It is a set of skills, each of which will be used in conjunction with one another depending on the situation.

There is one thing that we know for certain in life. It is the fact that, at certain points in our lives, we will be miserable. While different generations face unique challenges, it only goes to show that what we used to face in the past may no longer be relevant to our children today.

Even though we have so little control over the environment around our children, we can teach them one important thing: response. When faced with a steep drop in one's life, you can either shatter upon impact or bounce back by, according to Dr. Gregg Steinberg, in his Ted Talk, using our painful experience as a chisel to free our authentic self, to become the person we're meant to be. Though the situations children face in this day and age are unique, and unlike anything we have seen before, there are also many psychological and environmental elements that prove invaluable in the protection of children.

One cannot overstress the importance of developing resilience in children as early as possible. The sooner they grasp the idea and develop the necessary skills, the sooner they are able to cope with adversity, thus preventing long-term emotional traumas from occurring.

Different Approaches to Resilience

To help you create a way to develop resilience in children, you need to understand how resilience develops in children first. There are three main approaches to this:

The compensatory approach: As the name suggests, this approach is characterized by the countering of the negative influence of the environment with a positive influence. For instance, in order to protect children from the dangers of the neighborhood, parental supervision is advised.

The protective factor approach: This approach uses a more hands-on approach compared to the compensatory approach. Here, the parents employ protective measures to protect children from harm.

The challenge model is characterized by the quote, "What doesn't kill you makes you stronger." The problem here is knowing exactly what does not kill you. It is a tricky concept to apply because it depends on the nature and degree of the risk itself. For instance, you would think that a child from a military family who has to move from one school to another would have problems with socializing. In some cases, such transitions may teach the kid how to make deep and meaningful connections with people. It is the same situation, but there are many other variables that do not fall under your control, such as the child's temperament, intelligence, social support, etc.

While all of these models give you an idea of what resilience is and how it is formed, you need real-life examples to determine what it looks like. Before we can proceed to develop resilience in children, we need a way to determine if someone has resilience.

Resilience is something that you do not know you really have until you start using it. People do not know that they are very resilient until they see their peers collapsing under the same circumstance. Through this, we can see resilience as emotional insurance. We can gauge children's resilience in two ways:

- Development goals: A resilient child is the one who is able to meet developmental goals for their age, such as being able to walk, speak, make friends, etc.

- Adaptive Behavioral and Psychological Outcome: Children are considered resilient if they experience positive outcomes like attaining deep and meaningful relationships with their peers, academic achievements, and emotional well-being.

But these are just theories. Let us look at some of the most atrocious situations and how resilient children come up on top.

Examples of Resilient Children

One great example comes from the late 1990s in Romanian orphanages. No one really knows the situation of those establishments until it was made known by reporters. Children there suffered from an extreme case of neglect, deprivation as well as developmental delays. No one was expecting these children to thrive even after their situation has been amended. Those poor children were soon adopted into suitable and nurturing homes after. Many of them start to meet their developmental goals and seem to thrive. Of course, the traumas they suffered did not really go away even when they reached adulthood. However, what was impressive here is the fact that these children survived in the face of great odds and even thrived. This is a great example of resilience.

Another example of resilience in children is the 2004 tsunami in Sri Lanka. The tsunami devastated the entire country, killing tens of thousands of lives and displacing millions in its wake, among which were children. These children suffered great losses as they lost their homes and their family. Again, such traumas were not likely to go away, but some children managed to overcome this difficulty and thrived, displaying healthy developments and meeting their developmental milestones.

So, what exactly gave these children the strength to survive in such difficult circumstances? Many studies have been made over similar cases, and they all agree that these children only experience healthy development even after such traumatic events because of their solid mother-child relationship. This bond gives children the strength to withstand the negative influence of these traumatic events.

Parents could learn a lot from Michael Kalous' Ted Talk on resilience in children. In his presentation, he discussed some of the most painful situations that children had to go through and somehow came out on top. Among his examples was his own life story of his own traumatic childhood in which he had suffered extreme abuse and instability.

In spite of his unfortunate situation, Kaloud had displayed great developmental progress as we can see him today. When he was asked how he was able to overcome his difficulties even though it would have permanently marred anyone else, he pointed out his own five protective mechanisms:

- Purpose: The most important factor for motivation is a purpose. It gives value and meaning to what we do. It drives people forward in spite of all the difficulties in their way.

- Hero: A hero serves as a role model for children. That hero can either be a fictional character like Superman or an ordinary person, such as the child's father or mother. A child will turn to this hero and ask himself what the hero would do in this situation and then act. Therefore, this hero serves as a spiritual or moral compass.

- Refuge: When the going gets tough, we all need to take a break from the stressful situation and go to where we feel safest and at ease. Children need to have this place where they can calm themselves. This place is usually home, in which they can remain to cope with stressors at school. This is why you need to maintain a positive air in the house. Children spend most of their time at home and at school. School is already stressful enough, and you cannot do anything to change that. However, you can manage the household environment, so keep it positive to give children some respite.

- Solitude: Sometimes, being in a relaxing place is not enough. Children may need to be alone, especially after a hectic event. This place should be where children can have some privacy. Their room is a good example. Alternatively, the park or any other place where children can be close to nature also gives them the peace they need.

- Voice: One key principle of positive reinforcement is choice. Giving your children a say in the matter is important as they can foster their own sense of independence. They need to learn how to decide for themselves in the future. Plus, giving them a chance to voice their own opinions and feelings enable you to understand their point of view and need better.

Sources of Resilience

In order for us to help children build up their resilience reservoir, we need to understand where resilience comes from first. There are three main sources:

- I AM: This source refers to the innate qualities of children, such as their temperament, personality, beliefs, values, attitudes, and emotions.

- I HAVE: This source refers to external influences and what children have to work with, such as the family circumstances, the neighborhood, or the economy at large.

- I CAN: This source refers to what children can do about their current situation, which is a combination of the previous two sources and their skills, such as interpersonal and social skills.

When you classify all the resilience-building qualities into these three categories, you can easily identify the sources of your child's strengths as well as their nature. Of course, a child relies on more than one of the three sources from which they draw resilience.

It is worth mentioning that identifying children's sources of resilience is easier said than done. For one, it requires acute observation on the part of the parent to notice how their children remain positive and resilience. Another problem is determining which source does the child relies on the most. However, you need to provide the right environment to maximize the effect of these qualities, and this requires you to identify these sources.

How to Raise Resilient Children

It should come as no surprise to anyone that family is key to developing resilient children. Children spend most of their early life at home, so they are susceptible to everything that happens in the household. Therefore, it makes sense to cultivate a positive environment for them to promote positive, resilient qualities in children. You can do this by providing a supportive environment with open, two-way communication as well as employing effective parenting practices. With these simple methods, children are already well on their way to develop resilience. Other than that, you can have a greater influence on children's capacity for resilience by practicing pro-social parenting.

When it comes to cultivating resilience, it appears that the authoritative parenting style is most effective. Authoritative parenting is the best form of parenting as your children receive enough acknowledgment, love, warmth, while still being adequately disciplined and having the burden of living up to high expectations. The only downside is that it is the most difficult parenting method out there. In short, children are more likely to develop resilience when their parents assert consistent limits while also providing the children enough love and support.

It is also worth mentioning that practicing respectful parenting also helps build resilience and positive youth development. That means you need to support your child even though they may have different views, opinions, or perspectives from yours and allowing them the liberty to decide for themselves. This can be difficult for parents because children are prone to making the wrong decisions all the time. The key here is open communication. If you show your children that you respect their decisions, then they are more willing to accept the fact that your advice for them is for their best interest. If you respect their opinions, they will respect yours. This mutual understanding and respect lead to a very positive and meaningful relationship.

Other than what has been described above, there are many other ways you can promote resilience in children:

- Teach problem-solving skills: Instead of solving the problems of your children, which can lead to dependency, you can instead show your children ways to deal with their own problems. This allows you to provide role modeling as well as encouragement, further cultivating their sense of autonomy and self-leadership.

- Offer meaningful participation: Instead of controlling what your kids can participate in, give them free rein to pursue their own interests. Give them opportunities to engage in the things that they really enjoy doing.

- Develop responsibility: To develop your child's self-esteem and self-efficacy, give them some responsibilities to manage. That means giving them the opportunity to help around the house or take care of something. Giving your child responsibility can be difficult, but you need to do this to allow them to develop their mastery and sense of responsibility.

- Do-overs: While you give your child the burden of responsibilities, make sure you communicate the fact that you do not expect them to do everything perfectly. Make sure that they understand that they are allowed to make mistakes along the way, so long as they are unintentional and that they learn something from their mistakes. This helps your kids discover their flaws and help them improve.

- Identify strengths: On the flip side, identify what your children are good at and try to offer encouragement and support in those areas.

- Accept children for who they are: This is probably the most difficult thing for some parents to do, as they have an image of what they want their children to be. Unfortunately, it does not work that way most of the time. A combination of inherent characters, strengths, and weaknesses will drive your kid to become a certain individual, and you cannot do anything about it. Do not push your child in a direction that they do not want to go. Doing so only worsens the situation. Instead, encourage them to be their own person.

- Listen: Many parents out there believe that they have listened to their children enough. More often than not, we do not listen nearly enough to our children. They need your support and attention. Listening is not hearing. You need to pay attention and understand what they are really trying to say. That way, your children will understand that you truly care about them.

- Identify a go-to person: Children need a plan B or something to fall back to when nothing seems to go right. For this reason, it is advised that you have a supportive adult whom your children go to when they need support.

- Build empathy: Empathy is the key to deep and meaningful relationships. In order to help your children become socially accepted, you need to help them develop empathy. This can be done by teaching them how to tune into other people's feelings and put themselves in others' shoes.

Other than that, you can implement certain phrases to redirect how your children think to help cultivate resilience when faced with a problem:

- Humor: Here, you need to teach your children to see the humor in a situation. Laughter is the best medicine, after all. A common phrase here is: "Come on, laugh it off." Teaching your children to smile and laugh in difficult times is the key to help them cope.

- Hope: A common phrase here is, "I know it looks bad, but you will get through this. I believe in you." The idea here is to give your kid optimism, which is often what they need to overcome a challenging situation.

- Positive reframing: Here, you can say something like, "What can you learn from this so to prevent it from happening in the future?" Here, the idea is to help your children study the situation and try to get them to see the positive and possibly get important life lessons from the situation. Doing so helps them develop a more realistic view of the situation and develop their emotional flexibility. All of this helps them develop resilience.

- Contain: The common phrase you should say here is, "Don't let this ruin your day." The idea here is to get your child to contain the negative influence caused by the problem by taking its debilitating power. Your child needs to learn that they don't need to be perfect.

- Distract: This is quite a simple strategy and works more often than you think. A common mistake people make when faced with a problem is overthinking. Doing this only exacerbates the problem even further. This is often the case when the problem occurs suddenly. A common phrase used for this situation is: "Let's take a break." The idea is to stop the messy train of thoughts and allow the child's mind to slow down first before

- Handling worry: The idea here is to get your child to open up to the idea of seeking help. In some cases, the child feels that they need to deal with the problem on their own or that others would not understand them. Therefore, get them to practice seeking help when needed and make them feel included. The common phrase used for this situation is: "Who have you spoken to about this?"

- Acceptance: Sometimes, the problem is more permanent or is something beyond your child's control. In this case, it is a good idea to teach your child to accept the situation for what it is and try to make the most out of it. Here, you should say something like, "Calm down. Let's wait and see what happens."

- Perspective: The idea here is to teach your child how to take away the debilitating power of a situation and continue with their day. Putting the problem into perspective is also another effective way to deal with overthinking. Common phrases here include "It isn't the end of the world," or "It won't matter in a month."

- Flexible thinking: Teaching your child to think in a flexible way allows them room to change their mind. It is a way of saying, "This is a bad idea" in a gentler way. So, the phrase here is, "You could be right, but have you thought about…" This gets your kid thinking and further access their situation.

- Taking action: Finally, and perhaps most importantly, you need to motivate your children to take action. Sure, it is more convenient to sit and mope, but this neither improves the situation nor helps develop resilience. No matter what the situation is, ask your kids, "What can we do about this?" and let them throw some ideas around. In fact, it does not even have to be good ideas. The idea here is to get them to stop dwelling on the problem and take action because no problem is solved by sulking around.

Parental Resilience

Unfortunately, developing any qualities in your child is not as easy as telling them what to do. Because kids learn by example, you too need to develop your own resilience and teach by example. In short, you need your children to see that you are strong and competent as you want them to be, even when under great pressure.

Here, the greatest lesson of all is that of stoicism. In order to model resilience, you need to show your children how you see a situation. Most of the time, what causes people to be upset is not the event itself, but rather how they interpret it. So ask yourself how you approach any situation. Do you keep your head and remain optimistic in the face of insurmountable odds, or do you cuss and fume? Do you see a problem as something negative or a learning opportunity?

Again, children learn by example. You need to communicate the fact that there are areas where you have been resilient in your life. You don't want your children to see you as a superhero who can easily overcome any obstacle. Such an image will be shattered eventually. You want your child to see you as just another human being, burdened with many problems in life just like everyone else, but you maintain your optimism, get things done, and actually improve the situation. Your children will then understand your struggles and learn how to be resilient.

How Kids Develop Resilience Themselves
Now that you know what qualities promote resilience in children, it is a good idea to let them know about it, so they understand their surroundings better. This knowledge also enables them to take an active part in developing their own resiliency.

Luckily, many studies on child resilience in the past have highlighted some of the best ways children and teenagers (more on that later) alike can do to promote resilience. Those are:

1. Establish a consistent routine: Not only that, this paves the way for good habits to develop, but it also means that children have the opportunity to practice discipline by maintaining their daily routine. One day, your children will become adults, so you need to teach them how to manage their time properly before then. Make sure you communicate the fact that, since they are not getting even a second of their life back, they better spend every second wisely. Plus, having a consistent routine also helps younger people feel more in control and organized.

2. Accept change: On the flip side, they also need to understand that nothing really lasts forever in life. The change will come, and they cannot do anything about it. It is a natural part of life. Helping your children accept this face will prepare them, at least mentally. Plus, they will develop the mental strength to accept the transitions when the time comes.

3. Be optimistic: Optimism plays an important role in resilience in children and adults alike. Being able to see a positive in a negative situation can help people cope with the problem quite a lot.

4. Try new things: This involves stepping out of the comfort zone, which can be a very scary thing to do. However, the potential reward can be self-discovery and perhaps a new hobby. Taking such risks help boost self-esteem in children, not to mention autonomy and mastery.

5. Do volunteer work: One way one can help oneself is by helping others. Doing volunteer work helps children develop resilience, compassion, and empathy. This is one of the best ways to approach resilience development. Any volunteer work requires children to shift their attention away from themselves and focus it on the needs of others. Such an altruistic mindset promotes responsibility and autonomy. As an added bonus, your kid will feel happy with themselves because they have contributed to society and that they have done something meaningful. There literally is no better way to add meaning and purpose to your children's life than getting them to help others.

6. Get involved in extracurricular activities: You should also encourage your children to get involved in extracurricular activities in school as they offer engaging, fun, and rewarding activities to children, which will help develop resilience in children as well as a mastery for certain skills and promote social interactions.

7. Get a job: This is more catered toward teenagers than children. If applicable, have a lifestyle, a schedule, and a job

can help foster resilience as well as building a sense of responsibility. Teenagers may be able to get an entry-level job somewhere, and they will learn a lot of valuable life lessons. For children, you can give them chores to do as jobs, which will produce the same effect. Having a job promotes the sense of self-efficacy and pride of having responsibility and earning one's wage through hard and honest work.

8. Find and pursue a passion: We all have certain quirks that differentiate us from other people. One of those qualities is our interest or passion. Early on, try your best to promote your child's passion because their lives are more fulfilling and enjoyable if they are doing the things that they enjoy and find meaningful. A life of resilience and joy is only possible if passion is in the mix. Other than that, try to monetize this passion if at all possible. If you can, then your child has just found their dream career!

9. Practice self-care: One of the most important lessons of all is self-forgiveness. Things tend to go wrong, and they will go wrong one day. When that happens, people tend to bead themselves up for it and dwell on their failure. Some people turn to destructive behaviors to cope, which is not what you want your children to do. Therefore, you need to teach your kids healthy self-care behaviors such as getting enough sleep, developing good habits, eating enough nutritious food, drink plenty of water, etc. All of these activities

promote a balanced lifestyle that gives your kids the strength and energy to overcome difficult situations.

10. Try relaxation: Along that line, it is worth teaching your kids various relaxation techniques to help them keep cool and calm in stressful situations. This can be as simple as deep breathing to something more sophisticated, like meditation. In fact, any relaxation method you know should be taught so that your children can apply on their own to maintain emotional balance.

11. Be aware of stressors: Speaking of relaxation, you can also teach your children to solve problems by taking away the source of the problems rather than developing ways to tolerate them. In this case, stressor identification. Many young people are not aware of all the underlying stressors that complicate their life. For instance, your kid may not be able to understand that their lack of sleep and poor study habits are the reasons why they are doing badly in school. When you help your children identify these stressors, they can learn from their mistakes and know how to handle similar problems in the future.

12. Set reasonable goals: Having high expectations for something only sets you up for disappointments. Young people tend to feel that they are not doing enough. They feel that they could have put in more effort, and the results

would have been better. In this case, you need to teach your children how to take pride in their work.

13. Take breaks: Speaking of not doing enough, make sure that you communicate the fact that they need to take it easy on themselves. Early on, children feel the enormous pressure to perform well in school. During their time in school, they become very goal-oriented and are often extremely driven toward achievement. Of course, being committed and motivated to achieve a goal is good, but it is just as important to remind your kids to stay healthy by taking short breaks to allow their mind and body to relax between bouts of intense works.

14. Listen and learn from others: Children learn by example, and so do teenagers. Take every opportunity to give them guidance about anything you can think of. You can take your success or failures of others as life lessons. In the future, when your kids face a similar problem, they can draw from what they have learned and remain resilient.

Practice empathy: As mentioned previously, empathy plays an important role in resilience. Not only that it supports a giving and compassionate mindset, but it also takes the focus away from the problem itself, thus giving the child's mind some rest.

15. Form meaningful relationships: Finally, it is important to note that humans are social animals. We cannot survive on

our own. That also applies to social isolation. Life is meaningless without deep and meaningful connections. Therefore, teach your kids how to form such connection s with other people because their friends also serve as a source from which your kids draw resilience from in the future.

Bottom Line

So what is the takeaway message here? Resilience is a very potent protective mechanism that also happens to be a learned behavior. Therefore, even if you or your children are not very resilient today, you can start acting now and strengthen yourself going forward. There is still hope. While you cannot control what is going on around you, how you choose to respond to those situations is well within your power. Such is the power of resilience, and there are many ways you can approach it to minimize the risk you and your children face in the future. With a resilient mindset, you can at least secure your emotional wellbeing when everything around you succumbs to chaos.

Chapter Eight

Preparing for Teens

There will come a time when your beloved children reach that rebellious and most dangerous phase in their life. When that happens, you need to be ready. Sometimes, when you manage the transitioning phase properly, your kids will become very responsible and manageable teenagers, which will be a huge burden you can rid of. Here are some tips for handling teenagers:

Positive Parenting
Before we go on to discuss positive parenting and teenagers, we need to remind ourselves of one important fact: Teenagers still need and want their parents' support, affection, and guidance. It may not look like it, but this is the truth. Just like their younger selves, teenagers still need help from an adult figure to help them figure out life and overcome difficult situations.

You can help your teen develop an internal locus of control and their sense of mastery, which will develop their resiliency. You need to help them by empowering their sense of personal responsibility and their control over their future. Just being there for your teens can help them build resilience, which we will discuss in a later section of this chapter.

Other than that, the authoritative parenting style continues to be the best (and most difficult) parenting method for teenagers because it promotes two-way communication which teenagers want, while still offering you monitoring power over them. This parenting style has been shown to reduce risky behaviors among teenagers.

In this developmental period, parents have to face challenges much different from that of toddlers and kids. Teenagers find themselves in an awkward place between being too young to be an adult and too old to be a kid. They do not know exactly what they should do or behave. They want to control and independence, but cannot handle themselves alone. They are also self-conscious, frustrated by the change in their body, such as acne.

School only gets tougher for teens as time goes on, and the pressure from both the parents and peers do not help the situation either. In the end, they may become overly anxious and even depressed as they attempt to cope with stress.

Parents play an important role in helping teenagers relieve their burdens. Many of the problems mentioned above may require parental intervention, but getting there is difficult because teenagers tend to keep things to themselves. This lack of communication can cause problems for the parents because they do not know exactly how much freedom and protection their children need.

For this problem, parents are advised to use the "Love and Logic" approach. It involves two concepts:

- Love: Encourage your teens to be responsible and make decisions on their own

- Logic: Let your teens live with the consequences of their choices but show empathy for what they have to experience

Love and Logic method is an effective way to prepare teens for when they become an adult while being loving, warm, and kind at the same time without compromising your relationship.

Another approach is known as the Teen Triple P, which aims to minimize parent-teen conflict while giving teenagers the tools and ability to make the right decisions. It is effective in promoting pro-social qualities in teenagers, which can prove to be valuable when they need to avoid problematic behaviors.

One of those behaviors includes substance abuse, which is one of the worst nightmares for parents. The dangers and risks are real, and teenagers are the most susceptible because they can give in to the temptations very easily. There are many ways to protect your teens from getting involved in substance abuse, including:

- Getting to know your teen's friends

- Being a role model

- Being aware of your child's risk of substance abuse

- Letting your teen know about the dangers of substance abuse

- Setting boundaries

- Having an open and honest discussion

- Being supportive and loving

On Positive Reinforcement

We have mentioned previously that giving praise to teenagers should be done in private to avoid embarrassing them in front of their peers. They are old enough that they need to maintain their own identity as an independent person. Praising them in public undermines this identity, and their friends will see them as a baby and not respect them as equals.

Other than that, there are a few more things you need to keep in mind about positive reinforcement for teenagers.

Plan Ahead for Difficult Conversations

This is one of the most difficult things parents have to face with their rebellious teenage children. There are so many difficult conversations that you will need to have with your children. In this case, you need to get your points across without hurting their feelings. Therefore, think about how they might feel when you tell them "We need to talk,"

To prepare for this, make sure to prepare a time and place for this talk. As mentioned previously, take away the distractions and find a good time where you and your children can talk openly. Here's a quick tip: People are more open to talking about their feelings when you talk to them at later hours in the day. That time can be after dinner or right before bed. Just make sure that there is enough time for the talk and that everyone has enough energy to go through with this. Another thing to keep in mind is to give everyone privacy during the conversation. If each of your children has different problems, talk to them one at a time.

You also need to give them some control over the conversation. Ask when is the best time that you can talk with them and let them decide. Also, when you are talking to them, make sure you communicate the fact that they can always stop having the talk and come back to it at a later, agreed-upon day if they so wish. They are the reason why this talk happens, so you need to give them all the opportunity to have control over the situation.

If you show them that you respect their feelings and decisions, they are more willing to sit down and go through with the issues with you to find a solution.

Stay Connected
As children grow up, they become disconnected from their parents in one way or another. The things you two used to love doing together may no longer be a thing anymore. Some other activities you used to do together, which were insignificant in the past, are not more important than ever. Things like pancakes for breakfast, family pizza nights or Saturday movies, or any other forms of traditions that you used to practice in your house should be continued. Other than that, you should also encourage certain

spontaneous and casual actions like when your kid used to tell you how school went during dinnertime. Whenever these things happen, make sure you drop whatever you're doing and then pay full attention to your child. This tells your kids that they are important than whatever it is you were doing.

Respect Privacy

As your children grow up, you need to start to give them more and more independence. This is because either your children want to have freedom of their own or because you want your child to be strong enough to live on their own one day. There is no better way to introduce your children to do this concept by easing them slowly into letting them decide for themselves.

But the biggest thing you need to do is to give them privacy. That means giving them their own room if you haven't already. Teenagers have a strong need for some privacy after being under your watchful eyes for many, many years. You need to respect their privacy from now on. That means knocking and asking their permission before entering their room, not going through their belongings, not checking their devices or diary, etc. If you feel the urge to know what your kids have been doing when you are not watching, stop yourself and ask yourself how much you really need to know. There are many things that should be left well alone as a private thing between your children and their friends.

On Resilience

Adolescence is a very difficult time for both parents and their children. While the parents are worried that their children may be off doing all the things they shouldn't be doing, the teens themselves have to struggle with school, peer, and social pressures. Teenage-hood is not fun for anyone, especially for teenagers themselves. They have to experience a myriad of emotional and physical changes, and what their parents do about it will ultimately decide how teenagers will grow up. It is a confusing period between being too young to be able to do things on their own while being too old to seek help as a child would. This is the period when teenagers try to distinguish their own identities, which can involve risk-taking that can lead to traumas, social isolation, or even more serious problems.

Therefore, you should make it a priority to teach your children resilience as they transition into this troubling phase of their lives. But the problem is, how can you approach this problem?

Lasting Parental Influence

Some people assume that teenagers often rely on support from their peers and that parental influence becomes minimal. This is not the case at all. As teenagers develop, they still rely on parental figures. Parental influence is essential to help teenagers overcome difficult situations in their lives.

What you can do at this stage is to foster a sense of control and empowering your children to take personal responsibility and control over themselves and their future. When it comes to emotional support, parents should be more attentive than ever because teenagers will experience emotions that they never have before. Being there for them during their time of confusion and help guide them on the right path is crucial and has been shown to have a positive influence on resilience in teens.

Teachers, parents, or any other adult role models have an important role to play in helping teens drawing from their resilience that they have developed from a younger age. Teenagers need an adult role model who can promote hope, optimism, faith, and strength as they face obstacles in their development.

Teaching Resilience to Teens
Teaching your teenage sons and daughters resilience does not have to be a difficult endeavor. Many studies have been conducted in the past to study how one can approach this problem. Among them is Project Resilience by Wolin and colleagues. This study provided a structured format to approach resilience in teenagers that you can implement.

Wolin suggested having a group session with teens in which they can openly discuss their downfall, study their own flaws, discover their strengths, and build upon them. The idea here is to get the teenagers to reframe toward the positive by seeing the painful event in the past as a learning opportunity. They see those situations as opportunities in which they had to and were able to draw from their resilience to survive. There are seven elements to resiliency here that can help teenagers and even adults cope with life problems:

- Humor: Again, laughter is the best medicine, and it may just give teenagers strength to persevere.

- Relationship: Teenagers who feel that they are emotionally supported by their peers and family display more resilience.

- Initiative: Encourage your teen to take action instead of lament in the unfortunate circumstance.

- Insight: Develop resilience in your teen by asking questions to help them understand themselves better.

- Creativity: Encourage your teen to use their imagination as a coping mechanism.

- Morality: Teach your teen the value of morality, doing what is right, and standing by it no matter what.

- Independence: Most importantly, teach your teen independence, autonomy, or self-reliance.

Chapter Nine

Other Tips and Strategies

Other than what we have discussed above, let us break all of those down into a simple list that you can refer to for your own convenience.

For Positive Parenting
- Practice open communication with your child. Make sure you read between the lines and really try to understand what they are saying. Do not use criticism or sarcasm. Open communication helps your child to externalize their emotions and thoughts, thus helping you solve their problems.

- Support your child's independence, autonomy, individuality, and self-confidence by encouraging your child to try out new things and explore their surroundings. Just make sure to keep an eye for them in case they go too far.

- Do some research on your child's developmental needs and try to cater to those needs.

- In addition to being a parent, be a good teacher by taking all opportunities to teach your children valuable life lessons.

- Pay attention to your child as early as possible, especially in infancy. You will come to understand their normal behavior and how they communicate. This is crucial later down the line when you need to get your points through.

- Empower your child's resilience by teaching them to have a positive outlook toward life. Alternatively, you can teach them to be bold and look at the problem, understand it, and contemplate the worst that could result from it, and make peace with it, therefore draining the problem of its debilitating power.

- Encourage your child's development by reinforcing their capabilities, strengths, interests, and passion.

- Teach your child coping strategies that they can apply on their own when needed.

- Encourage your kids to improve their emotional intelligence by being a model. That means being a coach who demonstrates exactly how to be emotionally intelligent who can talk through issues rather than just dismissing difficult topics and hope the problem goes away.

- Make sure you communicate boundaries clearly. Make sure your children understand what they can and cannot do. Use simple vocabulary if you need to, but avoid making yourself sound cold or harsh.

- Take advantage of logical and natural consequences for behavior whenever possible. It is the best reinforce of them all.

- Whenever you spend time with your children, practice positivity by reflecting their energy and happiness.

- Encourage family activity and create family cultures such as Friday movie nights, Pizza Saturdays, BBQ Sundays, etc. to give you the opportunity to bond with your children as they grow up, as well as to create lasting memories.

- Have family meetings often, and encourage your children to express their opinions.

- Be aware of what your children are up to through supervising and monitoring in an appropriate way.

- Protect your children from the overuse of technology such as video games, computers, mobile phones, etc. Teach them to appreciate being away from the screen. Most importantly, make sure you limit their exposure to violent media.

- Teach your children the dangers of social media by pointing out previous cases and providing examples of dangerous online behaviors. Along that line, monitor their online activity just in case.

- Give your children enough coping mechanisms to overcome personal troubles as well as to promote resilience.

- Always parent with unconditional love. It teaches your children to love otters regardless of their flaws, as you love them despite theirs.

Handling Temper Tantrums

No matter how well you discipline your child, there will come a time when your child throws a tantrum. This usually occurs in the early stage of discipline as they are probably not used to the treatment. Children are more likely to throw tantrums at an early age between 1 to 3 years old. However, do not expect this go to away until they are older than six years old. One thing you need to keep in mind is that when your child starts to throw tantrums, it is a good idea to wait it out rather than trying to control it and failing miserably.

But first, we need to understand why they threw tantrums in the first place. They do so as a way to express their frustration. This highlights the lack of coping mechanisms. When your kid throws tantrums, you may be tempted to use punishment to quickly regain control of the situation, especially in public, to avoid embarrassment. However, this is not ideal in the long run.

One way to approach this problem is by talking to the child about the problem and explain to them, in a kind and loving way, why they cannot have it their way. For instance, if your child is upset about the fact that they cannot watch TV for more than an hour, explain to them that any more than that and it would not be healthy for their eyes and that you understand that they are watching their favorite show and that they are disappointed.

Another way to diffuse the situation is by giving the child a space to calm down. Such a place could be their room. When your kid is calmer, you can attempt to distract them from the problem. Giving your kid time to chill out is important for both you and your child because you also need to calm yourself down, take a few deep breaths, and reassess the situation better to avoid having your kids throwing tantrums again. While you are working out a solution to their problems, make sure to give your child a hug to let them know how much you love them. The hug can also calm the child down as they experience a familiar warmth, and it can reduce the child's frustration.

You can also adapt to the "Love and Logic" parenting method when approaching tantrum problems. The fundamental idea is that you must never argue, raise your voice, or excuse behaviors. More of the time, when their children start to throw tantrums, the parents get upset and yell, which only exacerbates the situation. Instead, you can go "brain dead," which means remaining unfazed by your children and instead show empathy and love for them. Consider telling your children, "I love you too much to argue."

Of course, this does not mean that you should give in to your child's demands. Love and Logic parenting is not permissive parenting. You still need to make sure that your child is responsible for their actions by understanding the consequences. When you communicate this fact in a loving way, your child is more likely to listen and understand the point you are trying to get across. Eventually, in the future, your child will develop their own internal voice, which they will consult to discover the negative consequences of their actions. This causes them to make better decisions in the future.

Other than that, here are some quick tips to help you deal with temper tantrums:

- Stay calm

- Do not yell or shout

- Wait it out – do not attempt to control the situation

- Be consistent

- Follow through with your action

- Be a role model

- Do not reward the tantrums – it will only increase the likelihood in the future

- Do not argue

- Do not escalate the situation

- Do not worry about what other people think

- Do something to calm yourself – do not get caught up in the heat

- Do not take it personally

- Give hugs

- Give your child choices

- Leave the area – do not give your child an audience

- Let your child vent and cool off

- Keep your tone and speech kind and loving

- Tell your kids that you love them no matter what

- Talk to your kids about their feelings

- Make your kids accountable for their action

- Empathize

- Distract your child

- Accept that tantrums are inevitable

Positive Parenting at Bedtime

Getting kids to bed is one of the biggest challenges parents have to go through almost on a daily basis. It is no coincidence to see that parents tend to seek help from others when their children do not go to bed. There seems to be no good way to approach this problem, and the situation is only made worse because the parents themselves are exhausted at the end of the day.

Many pediatricians can attest to the fact that this problem can bring parents to tears just by the sheer frustration of it. Up to 30% of children have sleeping issues, and their poor parents have to suffer the consequences.

This problem is much worse than you think. Children who consistently have sleep irregularities tend to have deleterious consequences such as anxiety, distress, marital problems, and familial stress, the difficult relationship between the parents and children, and issues in children's behavioral and cognitive functioning.

When parents cannot get their children to sleep, they may start to question their own parenting competency. After all, how hard can it be to get a child to sleep? Many people would assume it is not that difficult until they have to do it themselves. When parents cannot, they feel guilty about it. Some would get frustrated and start to yell at their children, which only makes things worse for both the parent and the child. In the end, some parents might just give up and decide to take the easy way out by letting the child sleep in their bed. This can be because they are too frustrated and tired to fight any longer. This usually only leads to more problems in the future.

If you allow your children to share the same bed until it becomes a routine, you deny them the opportunity to learn how to self-sooth and fall asleep on their own. There is also the potential for creating a lack of sleep and other marital issues. Thankfully, you do not have to deal with these sleeping problems by giving in or going crazy about it. There are many solutions to choose from.

First of all, you need to start to establish a consistent daily routine. At the end of the day, your children should feel relaxed and secure. If your child gets up, approach them calmly, guide them back to bed, and say "goodnight" in a calm and loving way before leaving the room. That is all you need to do. Of course, it sounds too simple. The only caveat here is that this takes quite some time. It requires repetition. Eventually, your child should learn that they should get back to bed at certain hours in the day. Of course, you need to be very consistent.

If you walked your child back yesterday, yell at him the other day, and ignore him on another, this does not create a predictable routine. This will initially confuse your child because they do not really understand the consequence of their actions. Eventually, they will continue to get up because there is a good chance they will get something good out of you one day.

Other than that, there are many other techniques you can implement to avoid bedtime conflict and encourage healthy sleep habits:

- Be consistent

- Tell your kids why sleep is important

- Understand your child's developmental stage

- Give your child a warm bath before bed – it helps with his relaxation

- While you're at it, use lavender lotion or bubble bath as both of them have been shown to have relaxing properties

- Give your warm kid milk or chamomile tea with honey – again, relaxing properties

- Make sure your children know when their bedtime is and when it is approaching – I suggest you use a timer to remind them

- Tell them a bedtime story – but make sure you keep the story lasting for the same amount each night

- Make your kids eager for the bedtime routine by making it fun

- Remain calm and speak to your child with warmth and love when they do not go to sleep or stay in bed

- If they do get out of bed and start to make some noises, calmly walk the child back to their bed, say "goodnight," and leave the room. You may need to do this several times at the start.

- Do not give in if your child asks to sleep in your bed

- Show empathy

- If your child does not go to sleep because they think there is a monster under the bed, do not disregard their fears and provide solutions (make things up if you have to, such as giving them "monster spray")

- Introduce your child to meditation and other relaxation techniques early on

- Play gentle, soft music/nature sounds/sing a lullaby

- Show affection

- If you must, dim the light

- Leave the door open if appropriate

- Make sure that the bed and your child's pajamas are comfortable

- Give your child a stuffed animal or blanket

- Set up a bedroom that is peaceful, tidy, and quiet

- Use a humidifier – for the comforting white noise and moisture

- Consider putting a fish tank in the room that produces soothing sounds

- Put glow-in-the-dark stars on the ceiling

- Alternatively, buy a glowing star projector – make sure it's not too bright

- Sit with your kid until they're sleepy but not all the way until they fall asleep – they need to learn how to soothe themselves to fall asleep

- Consult a doctor and see if your child has any medical issues related to sleep

- Maintain the child's eating and sleeping schedule

- Teach and ask your kid to think of non-stressful, relaxing things when they are trying to fall asleep

- Teach your child relaxation techniques

- Make sure that everything is quiet around the house around bedtime

- Make sure your kid has a healthy diet and avoid having her eat near bedtime because this will keep her awake

- Ensure that your child is not eating anything stimulating in the evening such as chocolate

- Make sure that your kid gets enough exercise during the day – they need to burn off the excess energy before the day ends

- Do not let your child look at TV, computer, mobile phone, etc. for at least one hour before bedtime – the blue lights from those devices will keep your kid awake

- Do not expose your child to things that they find scary or overstimulating a few hours leading up to the bedtime

- Do not let your kid drink too much fluid before bedtime and make sure they visit the bathroom first

- Avoid discussing emotional topics before bedtime

- Be a good role model by sleeping plenty of sleep yourself and hiding the fact that you have insomnia if that is the case

- Reinforce good bedtime behavior by rewarding your child with privileges or praises

Other Activities to Consider

There are many activities to choose from to help you bond with your children and understand them better. Here are a few ideas:

- Cook or bake together

- Go to the library

- Go to the movies

- Go to garage sales

- Engage in outdoor activities with them

- Build things together

- Paint together

- Learn a new hobby or skill together

- Set up and run a lemonade stand with your child

- Play music together

- Visit the museum together

- Go to local festivals, local markets, or other seasonal events together

Addressing Sibling Rivalry

Sibling rivalry is a common problem in every household. In many cases, it is not necessarily a problem because the siblings will learn to set aside their differences and live in relative harmony. However, it is a fact that they will attempt to pick a fight at one another endlessly in the early stage of their life. They will argue on a daily basis, and they will compete with one another, which can be a good thing. Healthy competition among the siblings can make positive reinforcement even more powerful, and this rivalry can bring out their best selves. However, that does not mean that you should treat this problem lightly. The level of animosity between the siblings can get out of control and becoming toxic, interfering with the relationship, and causing much trouble for the parents. If the parents do not do anything to contain this rivalry between siblings, resentment between them may develop and cause long-term permanent consequences, one of which is deviant behaviors.

Many factors come into play when determining the severity of sibling rivalry, and you may need to address each one of them in order to contain its influence. It is a very complex task because you really need to monitor your own actions and that of your children to understand how they play into the severity of the rivalry. Something that you should keep an eye out for is your interaction with your children, your relationships with each one of them, their genders, birth order, personalities, and especially watch out for favoritism because it is a huge factor. Moreover, sibling rivalry starts early on, so there is little to no time to prepare in advance. It might even start the moment your child realizes that they are going to be a brother or sister. Jealousy can start from that moment. Thankfully, there are many approaches that you can take to minimize animosity between your children.

One of the solutions is to cultivate a healthy relationship or healthy rivalry, as we have mentioned earlier, to bring out the best out of your children. That is if they are willing to be a sport about it. You can foster a healthy relationship by engaging the eldest child and letting them know early on that they are going to be a big brother or sister. When you do, make sure to maintain a positive and exciting tone, which tells your child that it is a good thing for them. The idea here is to get your child to be hyped about their new role as an older sibling.

From there, you can encourage bonding between the siblings very early on by letting your child feel the baby's kick or movement, or even look at the ultrasound pictures. Another activity worth mentioning here is to get your child to help decorate the new baby's room to create positive emotional attachment.

In some cases, the newborn may have medical complications. Maybe the baby was born prematurely or had other serious medical problems. This can be very stressful for the older sibling. The situation may require you to give more attention to the younger child who may trigger jealousy from the older ones. If this is the case, you need to talk to the older child and explain to them about the current situation, so they understand what is going on and why are things the way they are now. It is also worth keeping the older children updated about the current situation, as well.

Adoption is a different story altogether because you have some leeway to prepare your children for the new addition to the family. It also comes with its own challenges, however. For instance, you need to explain to your child how adoption works and try to establish a connection between your children. You can engage your biological child in the preparation process, such as setting up a new room, as mentioned previously.

If it is international adoption or that you are adopting an older child, then there are a few more things you need to do. For one, if the adopted child is still living in an orphanage, you can engage your biological child in establishing rapport by sending the other child gifts. It does not have to be anything special. Stuffed animals, toys, or even letters should be enough to set off the relationship between the siblings on the right foot.

Keep in mind that if you do decide to adopt a child, you need to take into consideration their past, which will determine their personality, likes, dislikes, temperaments, etc. that will influence how the relationships between the siblings will go.

Other than that, here are a few tips to help you end sibling rivalry:

- Do NOT label: As mentioned previously, labeling is never the way to go because you are shaping your children by what you say about them. Avoiding labeling your child when he or she is the only child is very easy, but you may unconsciously label your children by praising one but not the other. For instance, if you say that the eldest child is a good student, it implies that the other siblings are not good students. This can create a self-fulfilling prophecy in which the eldest child performs well in school, whereas others do not. This can also create animosity between the siblings, as well. To prevent this problem, only praise the action, not the person.

- Equality: Give equal attention and love to all children, and only treat them differently based on their temperament and unique qualities. That way, you can certain fights from occurring.

- Teach conflict-resolution skills: Encourage your children to settle their disputes on their own by teaching them conflict-resolution skills. Only get involved when things get physical. Children are more willing to cooperate and cultivate a positive relationship when they know how to make amends.

- Stay out of it: As mentioned previously, stay out of fights until you absolutely have to jump in. For example, when your children are arguing, do not interject. Only interject when they start to hit each other. By not intervening, you give your children a chance to practice their conflict-resolution skills.

- Don't take sides: If arguments do get out of hand and they start getting physical, jump in. Even so, do not take sides. Instead, engage your children in problem-solving.

- Equal punishment: Equality also applies to punishment. If your children violate the house rules, make sure to punish them equally. If you have a house rule to limit squabbling, then make sure that everyone who got into the fight has to deal with the consequence. That way, children will come to understand that it is in their best interest to get along.

Parenting Through Divorce

Divorce is one of the toughest challenges that children may have to face. Oftentimes, the psychological impact is worsened because children had to go through a period in which their parents argue constantly. They had to suffer through all of that tension and negativity in the house before ultimately having to deal with divorce. Therefore, it is no surprise to see that divorce can have both immediate and long-term negative consequences. Among those consequences are increased risk for mental health, emotional instability, relationship problems, to name a few.

However, how a divorce affects children depends on how it happens. In some cases, children will suffer short-term negative consequences, but not having lasting psychological damage. Other children carry negative impacts well into their adulthood. Knowing this means that we can start to seek out ways to help children cope with parental divorce.

As mentioned previously, different children have different temperaments, and their personality and family demographics also play a role in how well children cope with divorce. Again, the negative psychological damage on children already starts to appear well before the divorce itself happens.

Therefore, the lasting psychological damage may not result from the divorce itself. The source of the problem could be from the poor relationship between the parents and how they handle it. Knowing this is important as parents can prepare their children to remain resilient if things fall apart.

Divorce is a complex subject, and there are many reasons why it happens. All of these reasons can make it harder for children to adapt to varying degrees. Things such as poor cooperation and general animosity between the parents can definitely make it harder for the children.

Therefore, divorce or not, parents need to contain those debilitating qualities because they have a negative influence on children even without the divorce. Parents need to avoid exposing children to their conflicts, money problems, or any other problems, if possible. At least until they are old enough to help with the decision-making process, another problem that parents have is that one of them tend to badmouth the other, either in front or even directly to their children. This can turn the child against their own parents, which may serve to turn the kid against himself.

Badmouthing the other parent is more common than you think, and it is a way to alienate the other parent from the child. It is characterized by the criticism of the other intentionally in front of the child. In fact, the parent can just tell their child the qualities of the other parent that are not necessarily negative but can be used to alienate the child further.

This can cause psychological damage to the child because they would be led to believe that the badmouthed parent does not love the child. Moreover, the child may believe that the parent is flawed, which implies that the child is also inherently flawed or damaged. This can have a negative impact on their mood, self-esteem, confidence, relationships, and many other aspects of life.

This is not to say anything about the negative influence of badmouthing over the target parent's relationship with the child. If the target parent fails to address the situation properly, he or she risks losing respect from their child or even contact.

So, how does one approach this situation without compromising the relationship of the child with their parents as well as their psychological wellbeing?

1. Take responsibility: Negative feelings about your significant other is inevitable. However, the parent's goal at this point is to be their best parent when the child is with you. Practice all the positive parenting pointers above and avoid badmouthing the other person.

2. Stop worrying: The other parent who does not have the custody of the child should expect hostility from his or her significant other. That much is certain. However, you need to do your part and prove to your child that the other parent is trying to alienate you by being the best parent you can ever be.

3. Be a parent: Many divorced parents attempt to befriend their children during a divorce. This is not ideal because it can

make it hard to discipline or set rules for your child. Another thing parents should avoid is telling their children about their personal problems – more than the children need to know. This can create unnecessary burdens for the young ones. At this stage, you need to be a parent because that is what your kids need right now. So, set rules, enforce them, and be consistent with them.

4. Discipline and love: Especially after the divorce, the parent needs to assure their children that even though the love that existed between the parents died, the love that exists between the parents and children still exists. Some children are afraid that once divorce happens, they may no longer be loved anymore. Therefore, when feelings run high, you need to discipline your child in a loving way. Otherwise, they may feel insecure about the relationship. So, set up rules and create a daily routine for the child to keep them busy and focused on the things that matter in life. When you spend valuable time with your child, you show him or her that your love remains unfazed.

5. Avoid blackmail: After a divorce, parents often compete for their child's affection. This can create an opportunity for your child to attempt to bring you two back together. That is not necessarily a bad thing. At the same time, your child may choose the mischievous path and attempt to use your affection to their advantage by demanding things from you. In this situation, it is easy for the parents to give in to the

child's demand because they want their child to love them more than the other. Do not do that. Instead, remain firm, and your child will come to respect you.

6. Remain flexible: Children need a routine to follow if they are to have predictable development progress. However, when they need to adapt and comply with two different house rules, they will become confused, and your carefully-structured parenting approaches may become ineffective. Therefore, talk to your ex and discuss their house rules and routines for the interest of the child.

Other Tips and Skills

Other than everything we have discussed above, there are some more skills worth picking up today to help you with your parenting endeavor. To help you understand which skill is most useful for which age range, I have broken them down by the child's age. That way, you can correctly implement the right skills to meet your child's developmental needs. These skills are:

0 to 1 Year Old
- Child-proof your home and take precautions in other areas in the house to protect your child from injuries

- Provide enough nutrients

- Provide stimulating activities for your child

- Talk to your kid frequently

- Hold your baby and cuddle them to give them the warmth and affection they need

1 to 2 Years Old
- Keep an eye out for household or outdoor dangers when your child runs around, such as drowning hazards, poison, fire, sharp objects, small objects, etc.

- Read to your child daily

- Encourage your child to explore on their own and try out new things

- Respond positively (such as praising) when your child displays desirable behaviors

- Engage your child in fun and interesting activities together

2 to 3 Years Old
- Again, ensure safety that I have mentioned above

- Teach your simple child songs

- Encourage pretend play

- Read books with your child

- Reward positive behaviors with praises

3 to 5 Years Old
- Safety, again.

- Engage your child in easy household chores

- Discipline your child using positive punishment

- Read to your child often and let them choose which book to read

- Give your kid opportunities to make choices

6 to 8 Years Old

- Teach your kid about external dangers such as traffic and drowning dangers

- Teach your kid how to ask for help

- Engage your child in exercise, but supervise the activity

- Tell your kid about school and other important things in life they need to know

- Establish family culture and routines

- Make consistent rules about the use of TV, phone, computer, etc.

9 to 11 Years Old

- Ensure that your child is protected from dangers when they are riding inside the car, biking, skateboarding, etc.

- Teach your kid about the house rules.

- Make sure your child gets enough sleep

- Teach your child about responsibilities – start by encouraging them to save money

- Get to know your child's friends and their parents – it's important when your child becomes teenagers

- Talk to your child about puberty, risky behaviors, and peer pressure

12 to 14 Years Old

- Ensure that your child is protected from peer pressure and help them make healthy choices

- Respect your child's decisions, interests, and opinions

- Provide adult supervision

- Discuss risky behaviors

- Set clear goals and expectations

15 to 17 Years Old

- Make sure your son or daughter understand dangers such as sexual behavior or other risky activities

- Make sure they understand curfew and your expectations

- Discuss sensitive topics such as depression and suicidal tendencies

- Encourage and help your teen create goals and plan ahead

- Show affection – they still need it from their parents

- Help your teen make wise, healthy choices

- Respect your teen's privacy

Conclusion

Positive parenting is the key to a happy family. That much has been proven over and over by many scientific studies. If you haven't already, it is time to start changing your parenting approaches and adapt the positive parenting methods to maximize their benefits.

Positive parenting will only work if you are consistent. It will take more time and effort from the parents in order for it to work. In fact, positive parenting is perhaps the hardest parenting methods any parents can practice. However, great things do not come easy.

At the end of the day, you will have great children who understand and share their stories and problems openly with you. The air in the household will be positive and pleasant. It takes hard work to get to this point, but it is worth the struggle.

Even if you feel that you cannot do it any longer and are tempted to go for the quick-fix solutions, remember that it is never a good idea. When you are frustrated about your children, remember that they do not know any better. You cannot expect them to know any better. They want you to be happy, but they just don't know-how. If you ever need support, your spouse is there to help you. There are many large communities of parents who are more than willing to provide help and support should you reach out to them. At the very least, you can share some of the misadventures you have with your children and have a laugh with everyone there.

With that said and done, I wish you the best of luck with your parenting endeavor.

www.ingramcontent.com/pod-product-compliance
Lightning Source LLC
Chambersburg PA
CBHW070109120526
44588CB00032B/1397